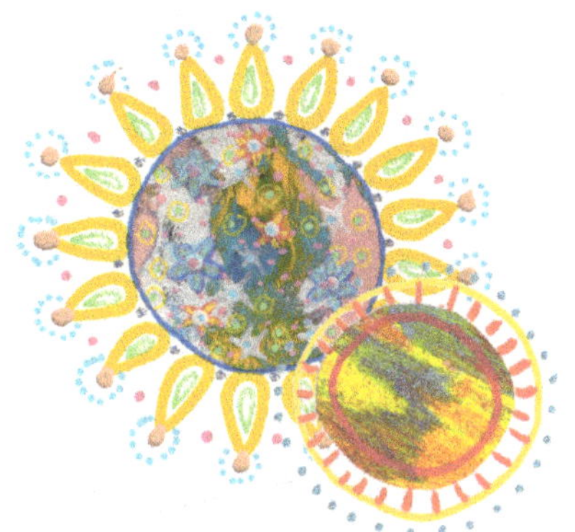

Soul Bubbles

Connecting With Intuitive Wisdom Through Animal Encounters

Written and Illustrated by Sabina Mesaric MA, ATR

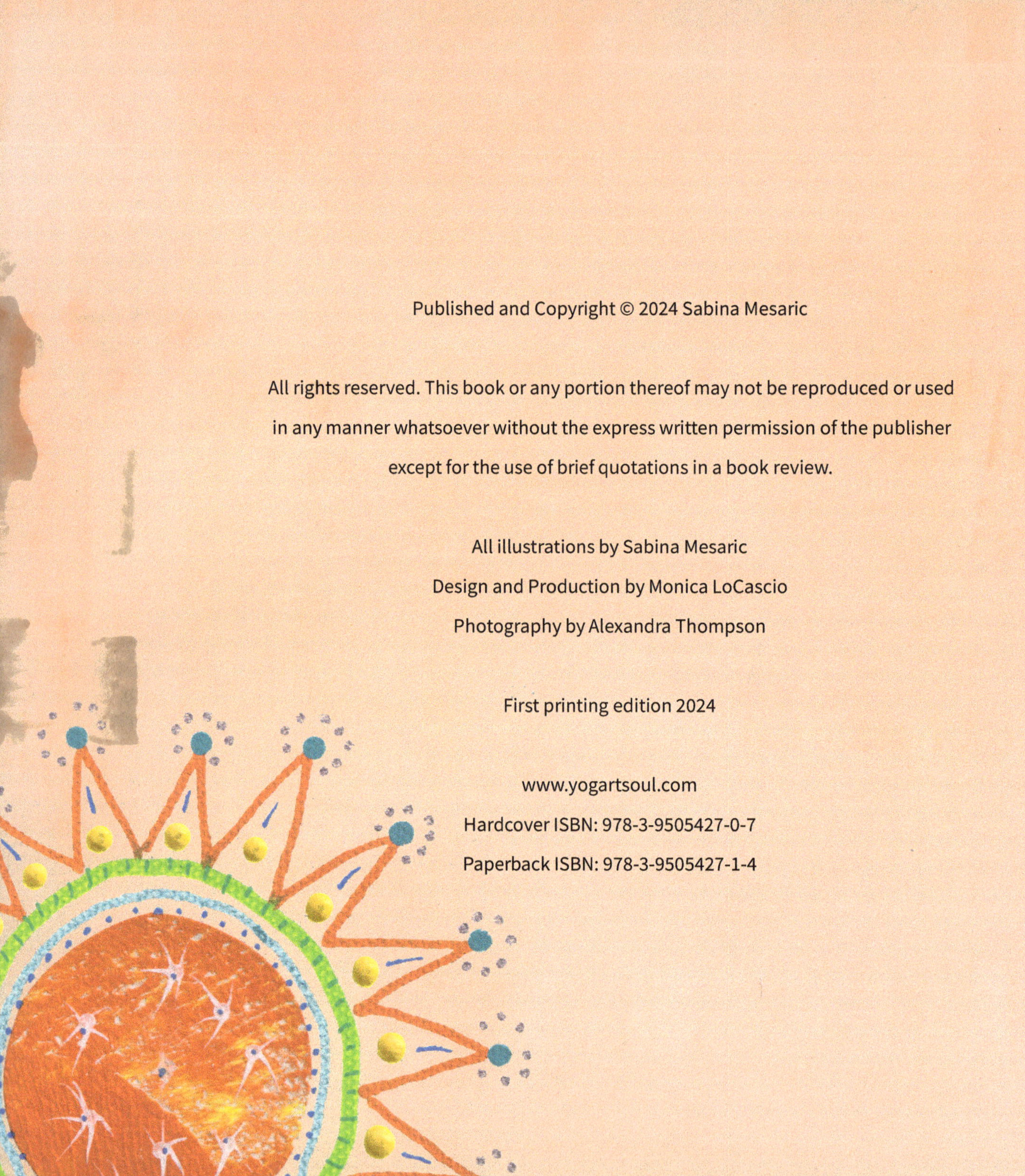

All illustrations by Sabina Mesaric

Design and Production by Monica LoCascio

Photography by Alexandra Thompson

First printing edition 2024

www.yogartsoul.com

Hardcover ISBN: 978-3-9505427-0-7

Paperback ISBN: 978-3-9505427-1-4

This book is dedicated to

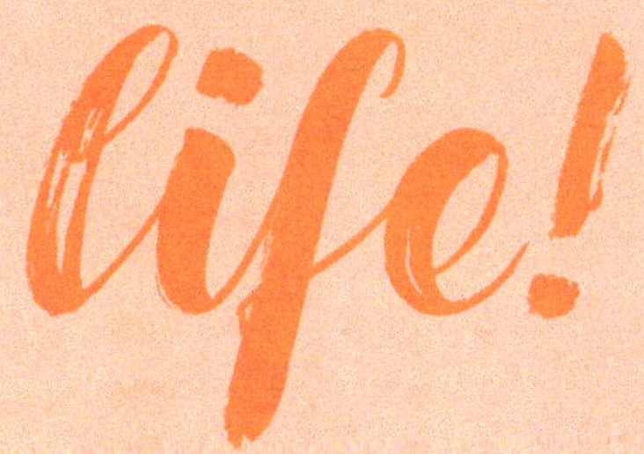

With all the ups and downs, you have taken
me to the deepest depths and the highest heights.

Never leaving my side, you give me wings when I need to
fly and roots when I need to ground.

You offer gifts and lessons, all in the service of my Self.
And through the past 52 years of being in your trusting arms, I have
learned to embrace the mystery of your magical journey.

Following the guidance of my heart, I commence
with curiosity and gratitude.

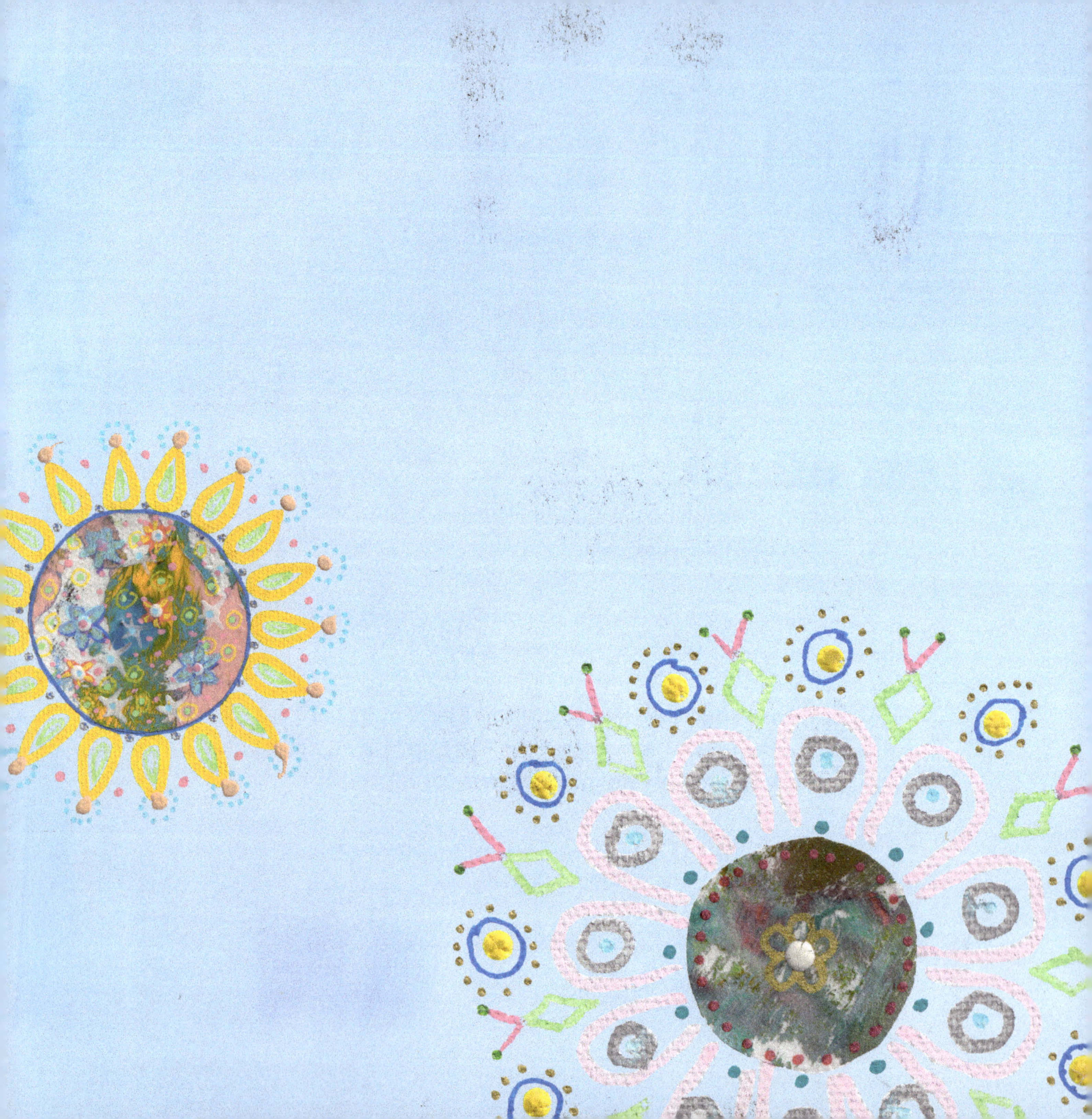

Contents

Trust the Timing

To trust the timing of our life is easier said than done. Yet when we mindfully observe and give ourselves time to reflect on events that may initially seem random, isolated, and perhaps even pointless, we become aware that there is a greater perfection to what is happening than we realize in a given moment. When we release ourselves from the need to control and lean into life with trust, we relax and can fully receive the abundance of precious moments given to us in the service of us.

Soaking in a warm bath filled with bubbles transports us from a busy state of mind, our thoughts, to a calm and peaceful place in our hearts, our intuition. While the tub holds the space for the physical body, the bubbles hold the space for the subtle body. By connecting with our intuition, we make room for the messages of our soul to gently rise to the surface, one bubble at a time, to be seen and heard.

Soul bubbles, like oxygen, are illustrated by the symbol O. While oxygen is essential to life - our physical body, soul bubbles are essential for connecting with intuition - our subtle body. Given the right timing and proper conditions, bubbles rise. By creating a space where soul bubbles, like oxygen bubbles, are empowered to ascend, we can transform our lives from ordinary to extraordinary.

So, too, it was with the bubble bathing otter who serendipitously appeared to me on the day I was designing the cover of *Soul Bubbles*. Swimming in a tub of bath bubbles, the otter, known for grace and curiosity, held a message to trust the timing of things. And as this particular soul bubble, with the image of the otter in a bubble bath, rose to the surface to join the other 51 animals of *Soul Bubbles*, I was once again reminded to trust the perfect timing of life.

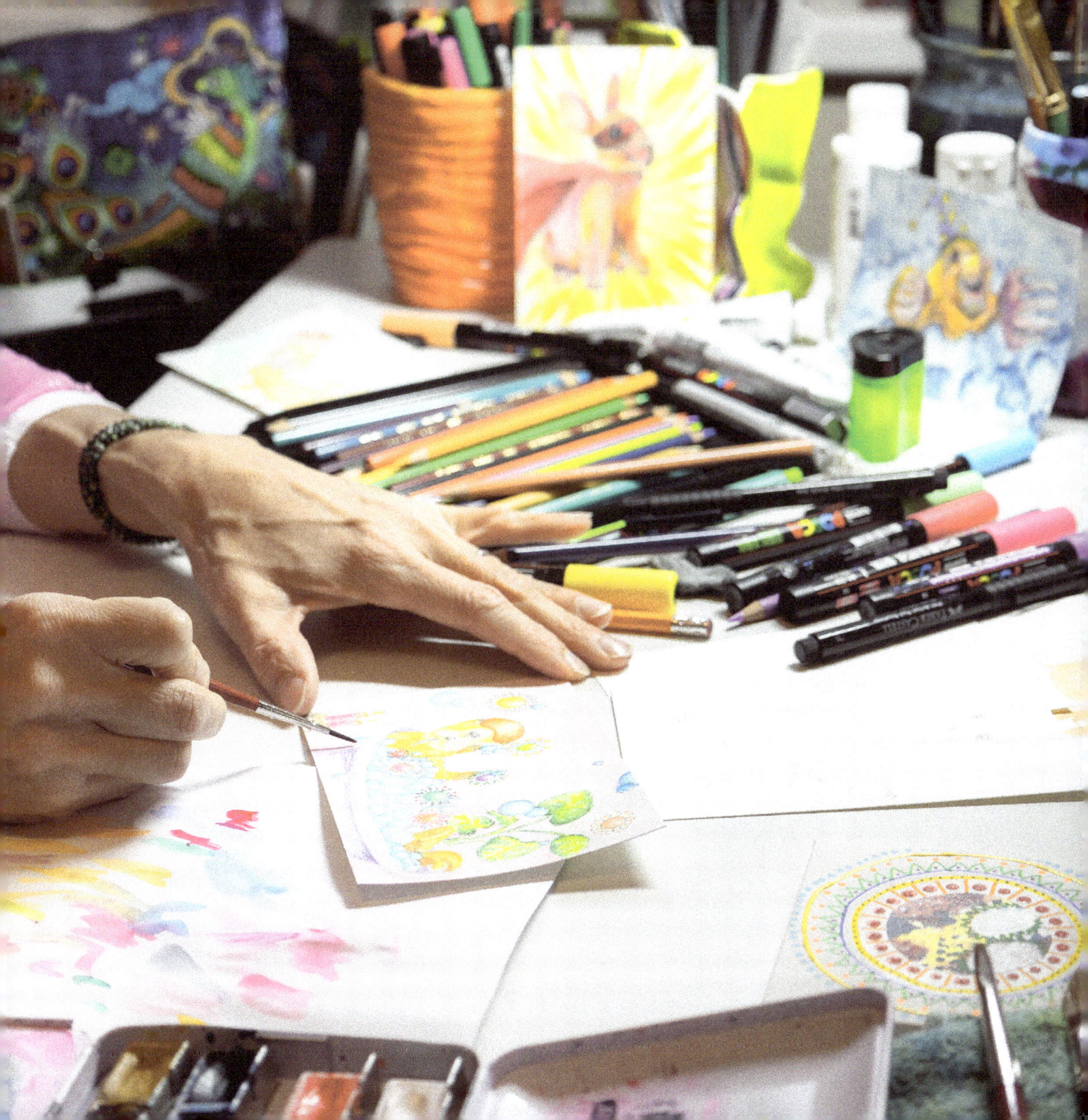

The Story of Soul Bubbles

Soul Bubbles was born from a challenge during which I committed to drawing one animal a day. What began with a goal of 30 days blossomed into a consistent practice which continues to this day. The 52 animal drawings and 52 accompanying stories in this book are a tribute to life and 52 years of being me. They celebrate the power of living authentically and creatively, and the beauty of seeing yourself and being seen for who you are.

The initial intention of my participation in a creativity challenge was to plant the seed for a consistent art making practice while improving my drawing skills. After 30 days, the cognitive goals of consistency and improvement were undoubtedly achieved. However, what emerged on an emotive level through this experience was more powerful and meaningful than I could have imagined.

Through the process of creating, I discovered that every animal I encountered, both in imagery and story, had a golden nugget of wisdom to share. The animal contained the nugget, and the personified details that emerged intuitively while drawing embodied the wisdom. As I engaged in the creative process, a dialogue with the animals ensued. It was through this shared story that I was able to process, understand, and discover extraordinary meaning in the feelings and thoughts of ordinary everyday experiences. Furthermore, I realized that by creating art and stories, I was also establishing a sacred space of stillness and connection from which the animal imagery and stories could emerge.

In order to expand the sacred space of intuition, the animals were originally drawn using a continuous blind contour line. The resulting imperfect image of this technique silenced my dominant and perfectionistic ego, thus establishing a quiet space in which the personified details intuitively appeared. For when given time and space, the intuitive wisdom of our heart has the freedom to ascend to the surface. Like gently rising bubbles, each animal made visible an intuitive message residing deep within. These magical bubbles, full of wonder and wisdom, became known as *Soul Bubbles*.

What began as a 30-day challenge
has now become an integral part of
my art making and yoga practices as a
way to understand, integrate, and find
meaning in the experiences of being
alive and being human.

Soul Bubbles arose and continued to
grow from a place of authenticity because
the bubbles are who I am, and they bring me joy.
Drawing and writing help deepen my understanding
of what sometimes appear to be superficial, seemingly
random feelings and thoughts of a human experience. In
this space of assimilation, I am able to transform confusion into
clarity, anxiety into peace, anger into joy, chaos into order, and doubt
into trust.

It is my hope that by giving rise and visibility to the bubbles of my soul, I can share their
messages with others to facilitate healing. Perhaps it's peace through identification; comfort through
community; clarity through mirroring, or joy through enjoyment. Maybe you are inspired to create
a space where your personal soul bubbles can emerge. Whether through validation, connection,
understanding, or inspiration, may *Soul Bubbles* be a gift that nurtures you and gives you exactly
what YOU need, dear reader. Namaste - The light in me sees and honors the light in you.

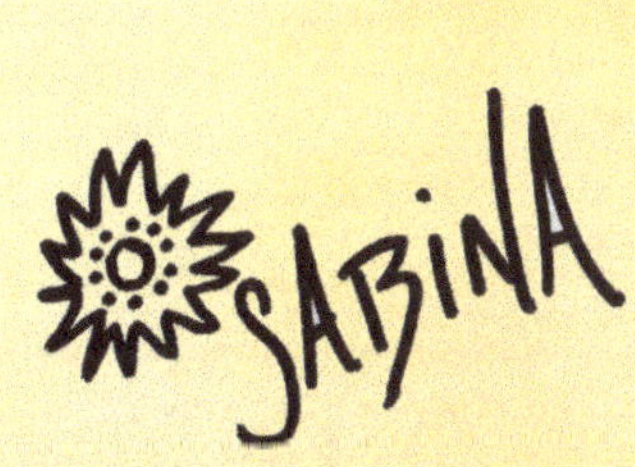

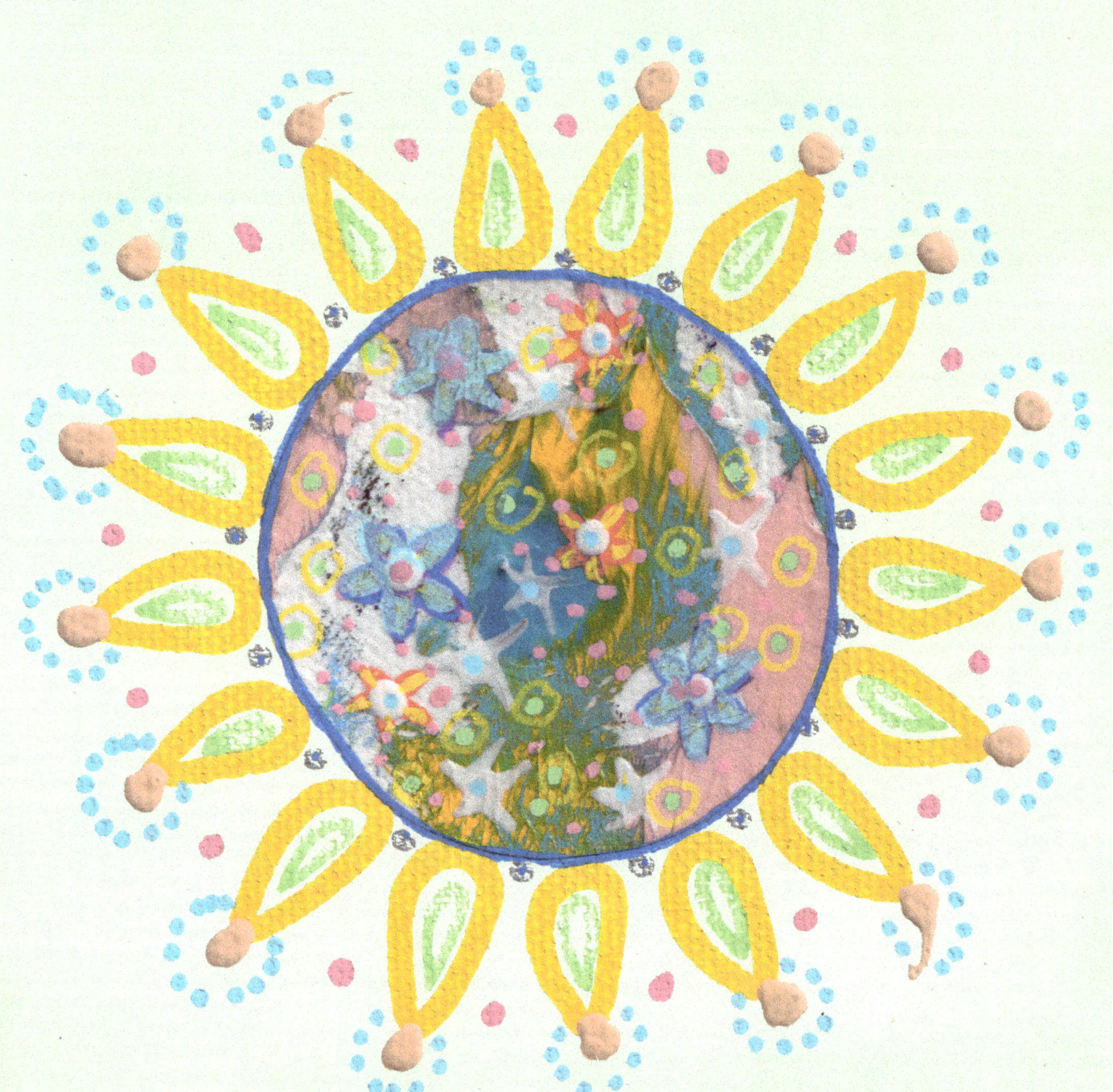

Ways To Use This Book

Life experiences and the animals in this book have taught me that when we pose questions to the universe, we always receive an answer. Although the answers may come to us in forms different from what we imagine, when we open ourselves up to receiving, the universe will fill this spaciousness with exactly what we need.

And so too it is with this book. The golden nugget of wisdom delivered by each animal messenger in *Soul Bubbles* will come to you, giving you what you need at the moment you need it. Some stories may even contain multiple nuggets. By rereading them at different times, you will discover that the messages also magically vary. What is essential is to create a space in which you can open yourself up to receiving the gift.

So what does this look like for you? There are unlimited ways in which you can use the book, and of course, there is no right or wrong way to enjoy and engage with it. Trust and do what feels right for you.

The following pages offer a few suggestions and ways that I have found work for me.

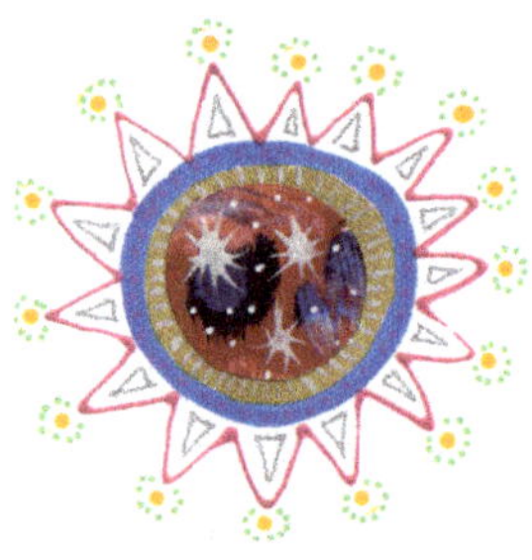

Intuitive Messengers

Hold the book in your hands. Close your eyes and tune in using the phrase "what do I need to know and remember for today?" Allow your heart to guide you and intuitively open the page that will reveal what you need. Let the story and the image be your support and guide for the day.

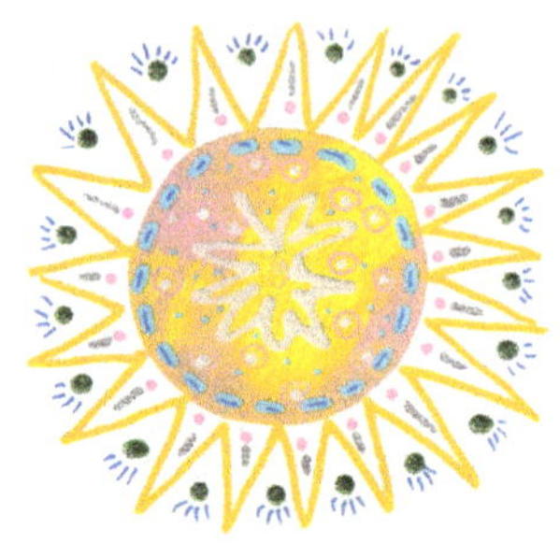

Sequential Seeker

Read one story a day sequentially. Observe the serendipitous alignment of the message with your natural life flow.

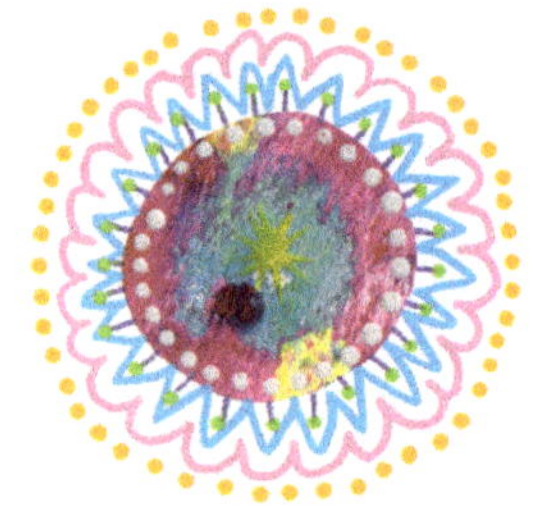

Your Inner Animal

Tune in and invite an animal to bubble up from your soul. Take time to visualize and connect with them. Then using the Animal Tribute pages in the back of the book, find your animal. Go to that animal's image and story to receive the gift of their message.

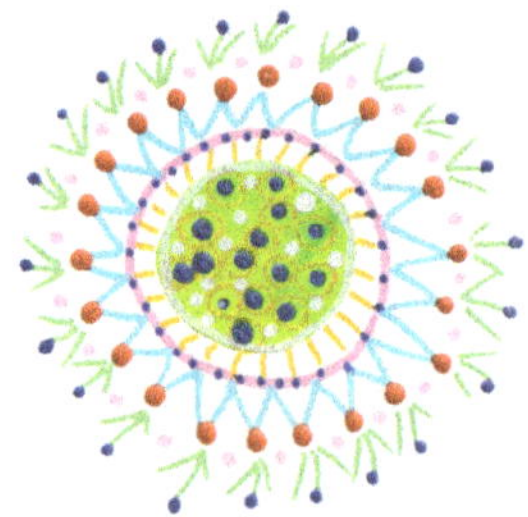

In Your World

When an animal appears to you in your outer world, use *Soul Bubbles* as an inquiry reference to discover why a particular animal visited you and the message they have to share.

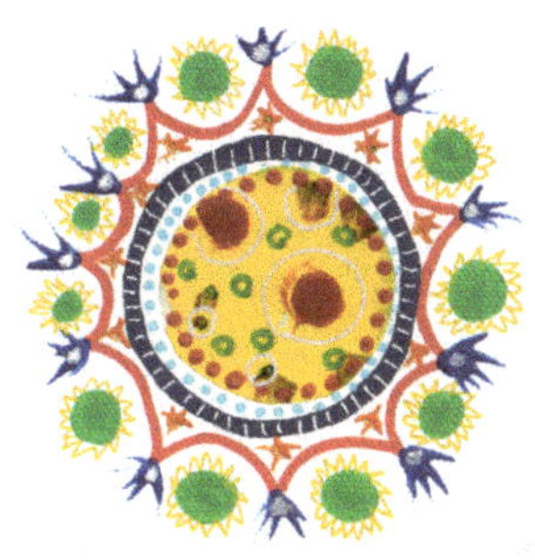

Creative Inspiration

Be inspired to tune in and visualize your own inner animal. Draw them using one continuous line without looking at your paper. In the space of imperfection that ensues, allow the golden nugget(s) of wisdom to emerge through the details you add. Then write a story inspired by the dialogue you shared with your animal during the creative process.

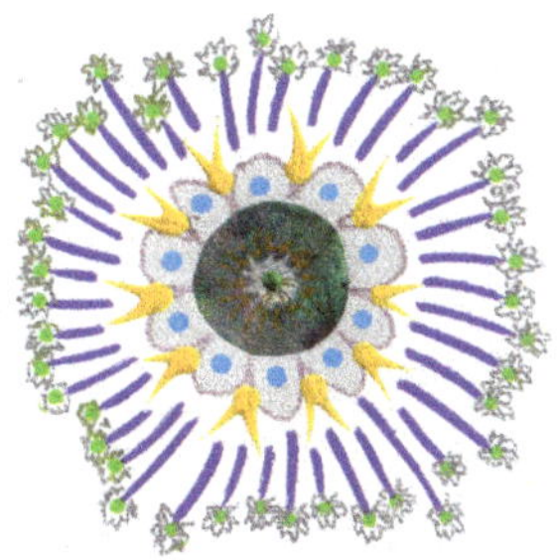

Dive Deep

Of course, you can fully immerse yourself in one sitting. Dive deep as you read Soul Bubbles from cover to cover.

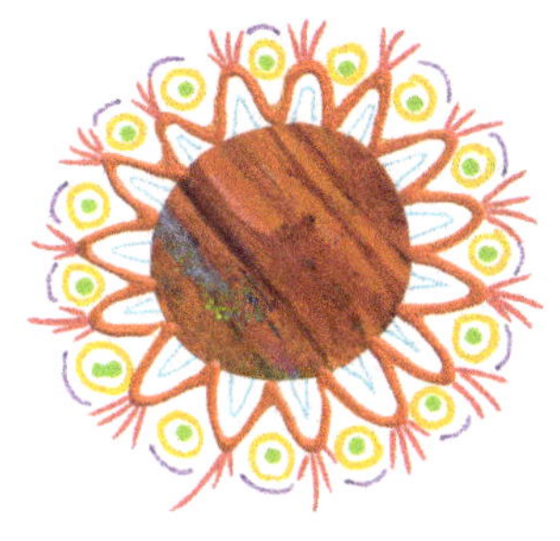

Notice and Discover

Be inspired to notice and find the extraordinary in the ordinary experiences of your daily life.

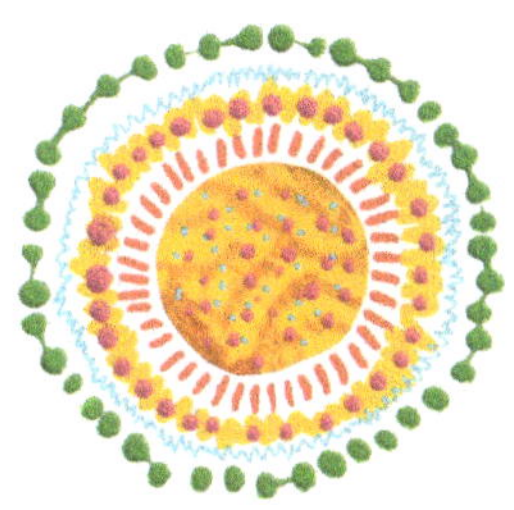

However you choose to engage with *Soul Bubbles*, may it nourish you with exactly what you need in the moment you need it most. The artist Georgia O'Keeffe once said, "Nobody sees a flower, they haven't the time and to see takes time…." With the intention of encouraging viewers to slow down and notice, she painted the flowers close-up.

Soul Bubbles is my invitation for you to take the time to create space in your ordinary day so that you, too, may discover and explore with curiosity and gratitude the extraordinary that is waiting to be experienced by you and for you!

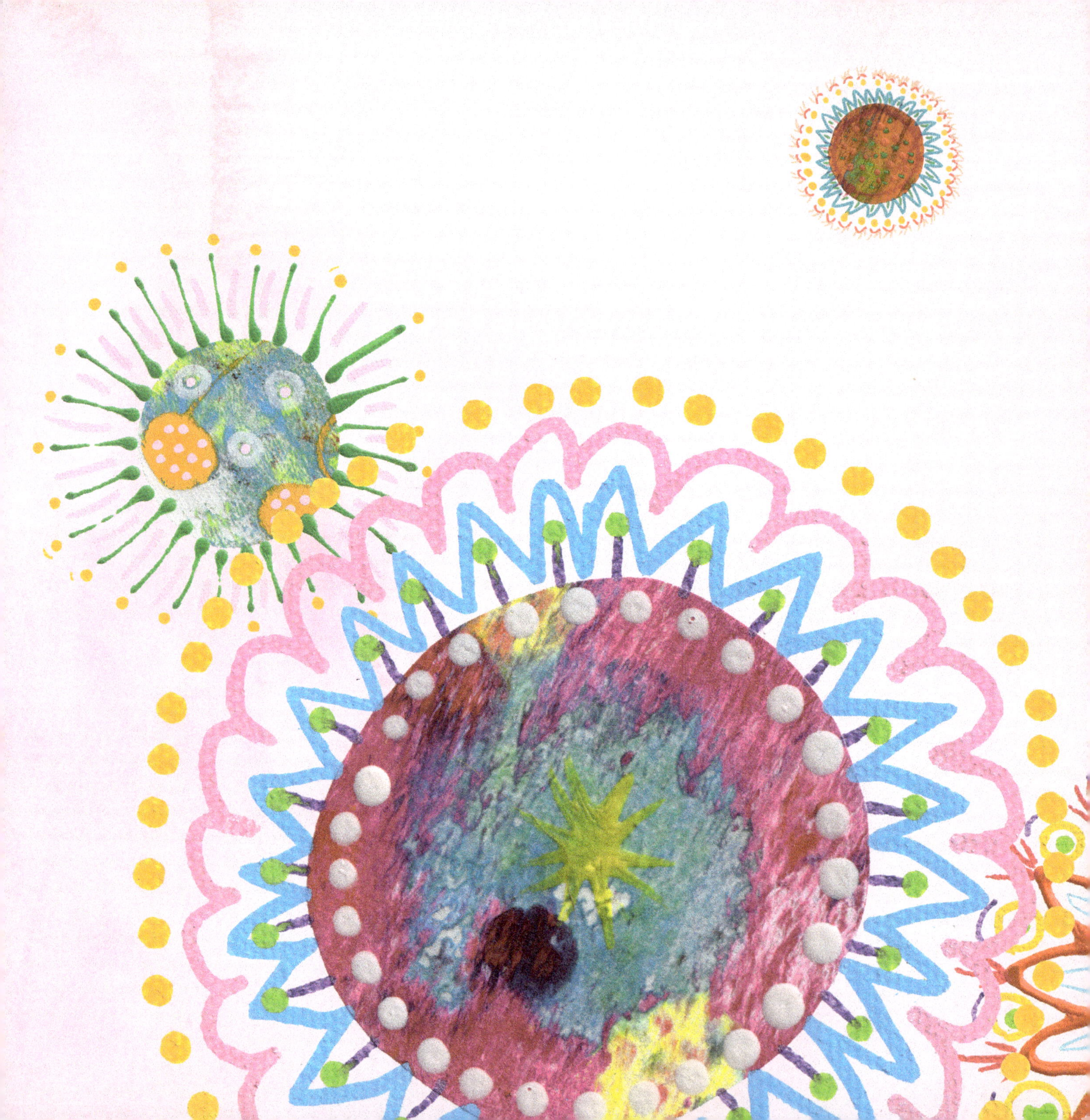

Turtle Teacher

Teachers come in various forms and show up in our lives at different times and places. Often, the biggest and most important lessons are shared with us by the smallest, unassuming teachers at seemingly random moments and locations.

A turtle basking in the sun on a fallen tree limb, unbeknownst to herself, becomes my teacher on a morning run. With racing feet and pulse, I am stopped in my tracks, mesmerized by the aura of slowness that surrounds this beautiful being. The gentle movement of extremities and the steady rise and fall of the mandible convey a mindful presence, a feeling of peace and calm, that I laboriously try to create in my life. Even when an unexpected 'wrong' move sends the turtle bombshelling into the water, she resumes her moment in the sun, untethered by the prior event.

I am reminded of the phrase "when pigs fly," an expression of impossibility, and I think to myself, "when turtles fly," I too will live with a mastery of slowness. Looking at the blue water below mirroring the blue sky above, I realize water and sky, swimming and flying, are really not so different, and that impossibility and possibility perhaps are in the eye of the beholder as well.

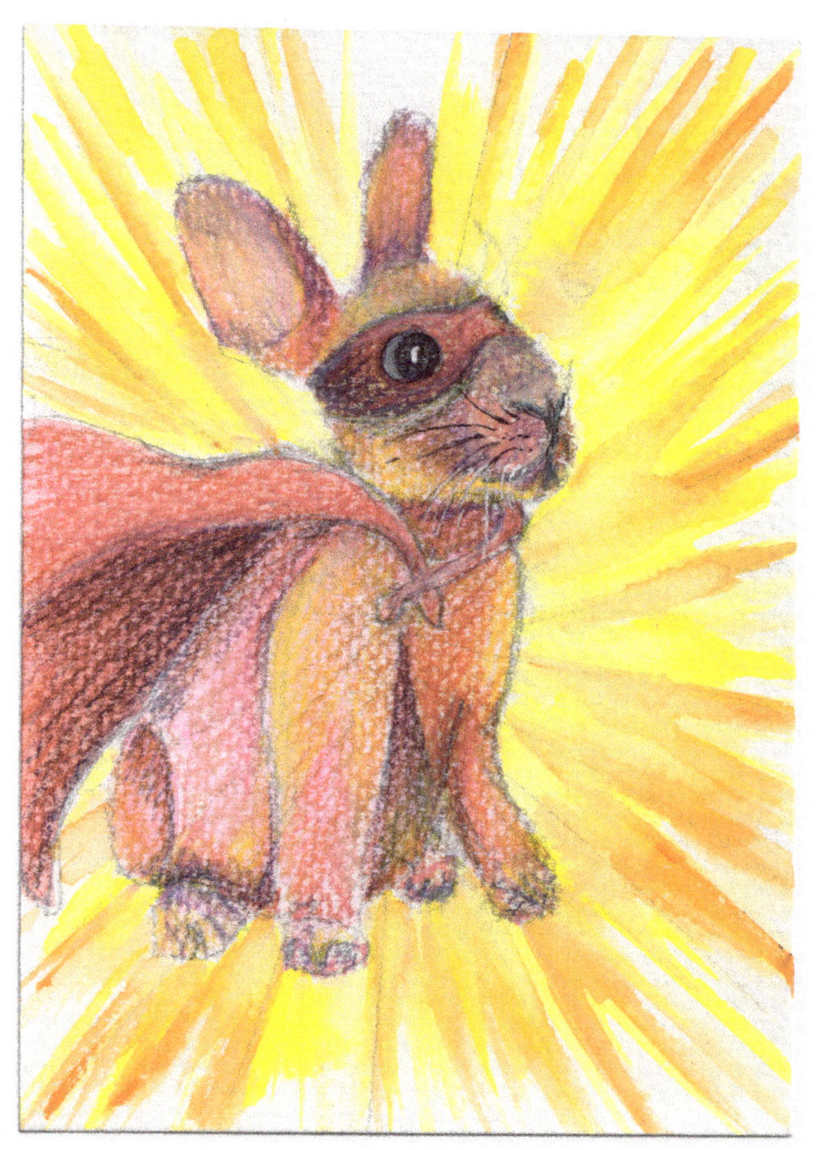

What's Your Superpower?

We all grow up with the presence of superheroes in our lives. Although every generation has their own pop culture version, the essence of these figures and the purpose they serve remains a constant throughout time and place. Superheroes are a personification of our hidden thoughts, feelings, and desires, which Carl Jung defines as the 'collective unconscious.' A hero, as cited in the Oxford Languages Dictionary, is "a person who is admired for their courage, outstanding achievements, or noble qualities," while a superhero is described as "a fictional character with superhuman powers."

Through social conditioning of the media and popular culture, we learn to admire a hero (super or non-super) for who they are and find ourselves in awe of the powers they possess. We dream of being like them and imagine ourselves having the magical superpowers they possess. Beginning at an early age, we are therefore conditioned to focus our personal development on external and often fictional characters rather than looking inward to connect with the hero inside ourselves and tap into the superpowers that we possess.

We all have something that we are good at that makes us unique and defines our purpose. Like magicians surprising their audience with the seemingly unimaginable act of pulling a rabbit out of the hat, we, too, need to reveal the hidden strength, talent, or gift that is our superpower to the world. Be your own superhero and hero. The world needs your unique superpower. As succinctly stated in the quote by the artist Pablo Picasso, "The meaning of life is to find your gift. The purpose of life is to give it away." What is YOUR superpower?

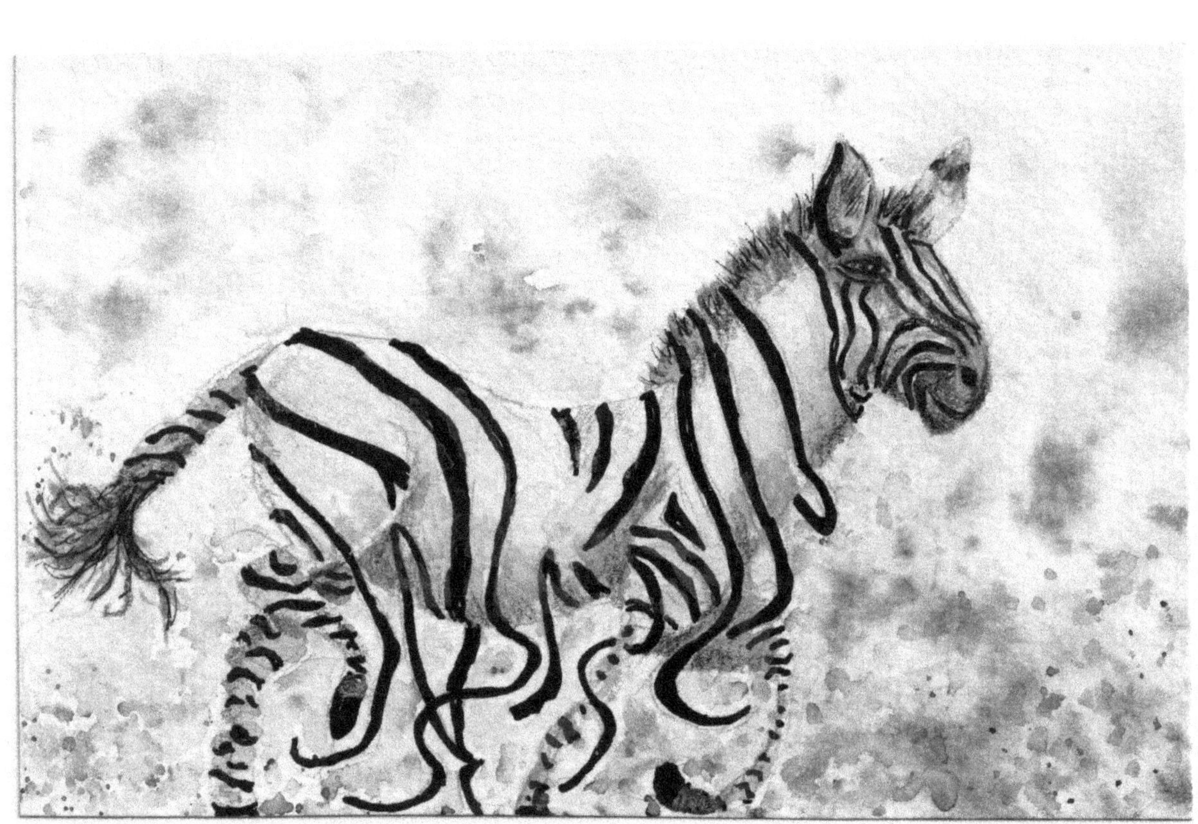

Black and White Thinking

Right or wrong. Yes or No. Black or white. There is clarity, precision, structure, and thus a feeling of safety in clearly defined contrasting opposites.

At first glance, the black and white stripes of a zebra mirror these polarities. But zoom into the light and shadow, the subtle values of gray visible under the belly; in the hair of the mane; the tip of the tail; the cavity of the eyes; the underside of the neck. Is that not where true beauty, originality, and mystery reside? Are the perfect stripes not just a grid constructed by our thinking, boxed up, and filed away by our ego with the best intention of keeping us safe?

What would happen if we allowed the binding ties of black and white thinking to unravel? Would we truly come undone? Would we feel naked and insecure, uncertain about how the limitlessness of gray values would be received by others? Or would we feel relieved and free? No longer needing to hoard our precious and superficially limited energy to hold it all together, we have the ability to share our infinite energy as we dance and shake it all loose.

The research of neurologist Robert Sapolsky shows us that zebras dissipate stress by shaking it off and returning to the moment. Using this technique ourselves, we too can let go of our black and white thinking and uncover the mystery and magic hidden in our personal palette of gray. So, abandon the perfection, predictability, and false security of your stripes, your limiting beliefs, for they are merely an illusion that is binding and keeping you from revealing your authentic Self.

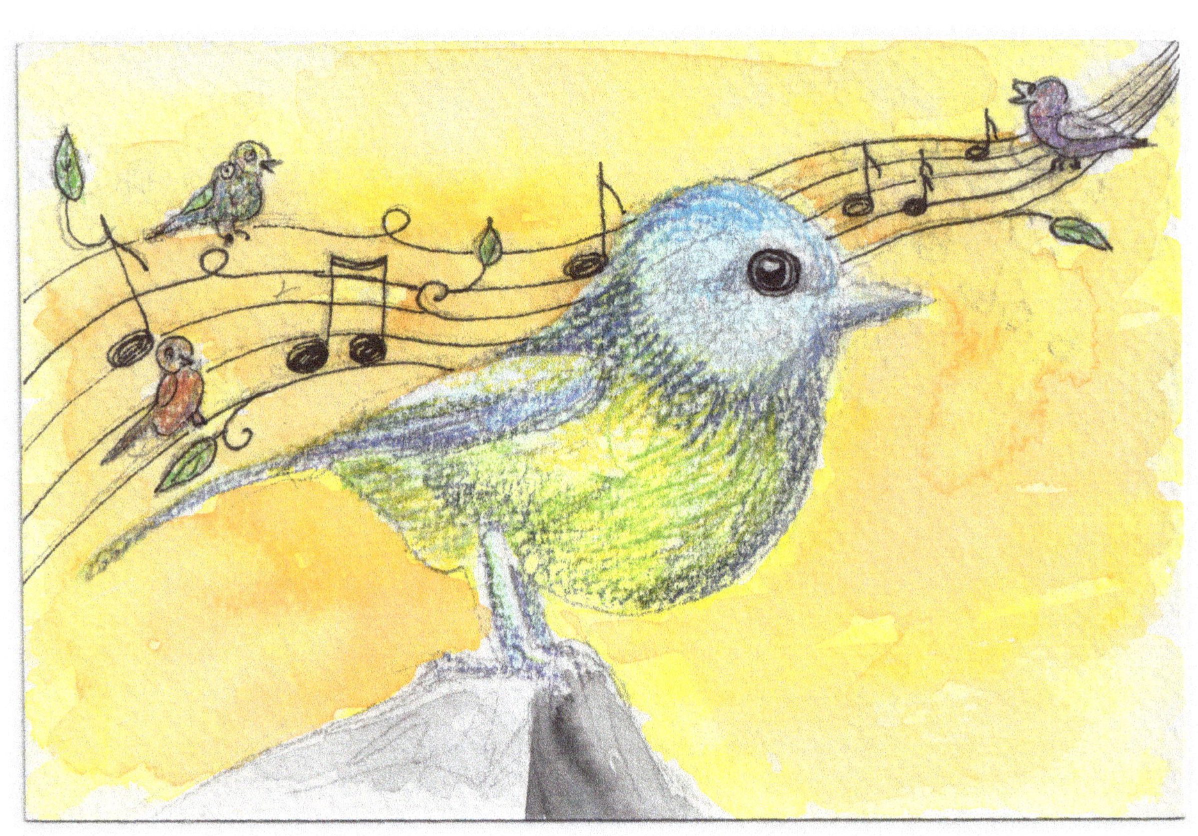

Tuning In

Living in an oversaturated, over-stimulated, overcrowded 21st century digitalized world can leave us with heads spinning, minds racing, and ears buzzing. Finding ourselves in a state of overwhelm, we yearn to shut down, tune out, or completely turn off the overabundance of input surrounding us. Yet, our habitual modus operandi keeps us unconsciously turning up the volume, seeking more input to feed our digital addiction in the hopes of inundating ourselves to the point of blurry disillusion.

What would happen if we reversed the flow of energy input, and instead of tuning out due to overload, we mindfully tuned in? By taking the time to connect and listen, we can truly hear the song that's in our hearts. These initially quiet individual stirrings will eventually evolve into the most beautifully orchestrated and harmonizing sequence of notes - your personal and original musical compilation that signifies you.

Bird songs are a beautiful way to fine-tune our listening skills. Bird songs ring throughout the world. Their melodies soothe, calm, and open our hearts because music transgresses the boundaries of language. And as we listen, we discover that they wash away the mind chatter, the lyrics in our brain and replace them with a melody that carries the messages of our hearts.

Nature provides the notes of a bird song when we slow down to stop and listen. We need only be aware enough to pick out the individual notes. Like letters of the alphabet that, when arranged, create a word, our mantras also become a way to express the stirrings of our hearts to reveal the messages and wisdom of our souls.

Birds will always sing. It is up to us to make the choice to slow down enough to stop and listen to their songs so that we may be inspired to connect and live according to our heart's songs.

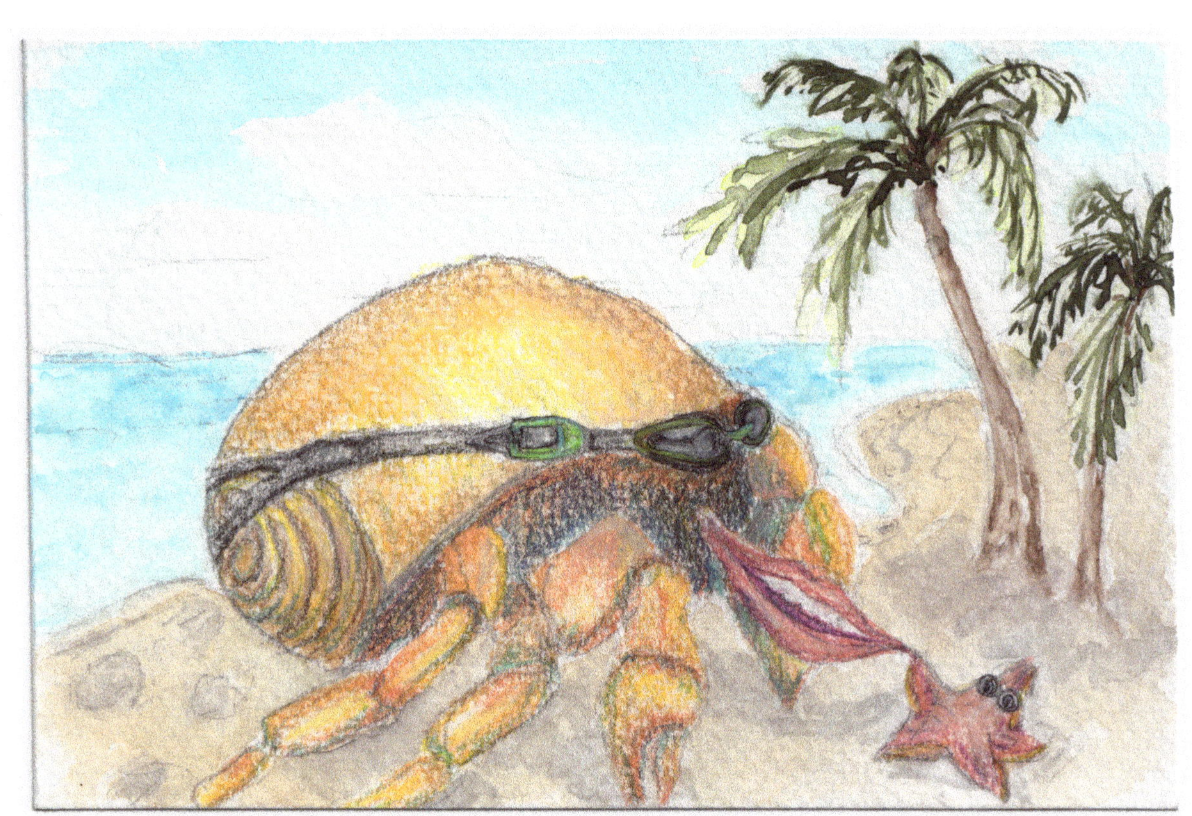

Sharing a Smile

The smile is an instinctive and fairly effortless facial expression. Perhaps the most universal form of communication among human beings, it can also serve as a mask, a shell of protection from pain, loneliness, and dis-ease living on the inside. Like the shell of a crab, we can wear our smile as a suit of armor. Yet, while the shell armor offers us safety and comfort, it also limits expansion.

So, what happens when we outgrow our smile shell or a mask conceals it due to a pandemic? When the smile no longer serves us or ceases to exist? Does our smile, like a crab without a shell, pass away?

Like a cap and goggles used by swimmers to protect hair and eyes, their ease of use is contingent upon the environment in which they are implemented. The cap prevents hair from dragging in the water, but on land, it feels tight, uncomfortable, and restrictive. Goggles aid a swimmer to see clearly underwater but obstruct vision on land.

Similarly, our smile is a tool, a precious gift that supports us. Sharing it with awareness and knowing when to wear it and when to remove it is key, for we must continually evaluate whether our smile truly serves us and when it is hindering us from showing up authentically.

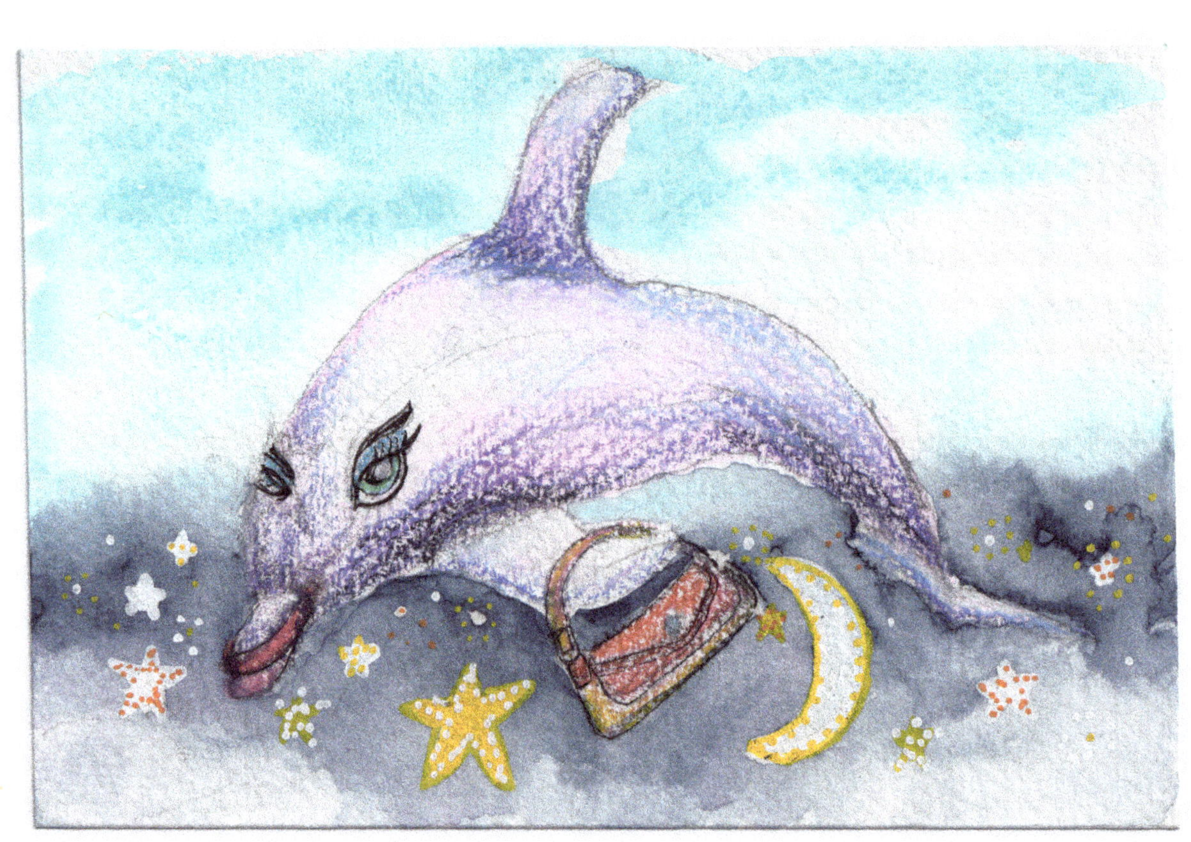

Diving into the Night

Sometimes it just feels so good to bedazzle ourselves, slip into our finest attire, pull out the mini handbag to lighten our load, and hit the town. Slipping out of our well-worn favorite attire and leaving the familiar surroundings of our home, we break through the often invisible barriers of our personally limiting zone of comfort.

Dolphins jump in and out of the water for playfulness, communication, navigation, or simply to show off. For us, jumping out and diving in is like taking a leap of faith. We place our trust in something greater than ourselves. We are energized with anticipation and excitement, finding ourselves filled with confidence as we head into unknown waters. After the initial dive, that first step in a new direction, we feel encouraged because we have tapped into our well of inner courage. Jumping and diving, every leap enables us to dive deeper into the night and glide through its darkness. We discover that the light of the stars shines brighter and brighter the deeper and darker the sky becomes.

It is in this moment that we realize all the external accessories we found necessary to bedazzle ourselves with at the beginning are and always have been part of us. For who we truly are, radiating light, is mirrored by the sparkling stars and moon of the nighttime sky surrounding us. As we leap and dive over and over again, we find ourselves aligning and moving in harmony with the universe, becoming part of something bigger. And it is through this connection to something greater than ourselves that we feel a sense of purpose and realize our life is truly dazzling!

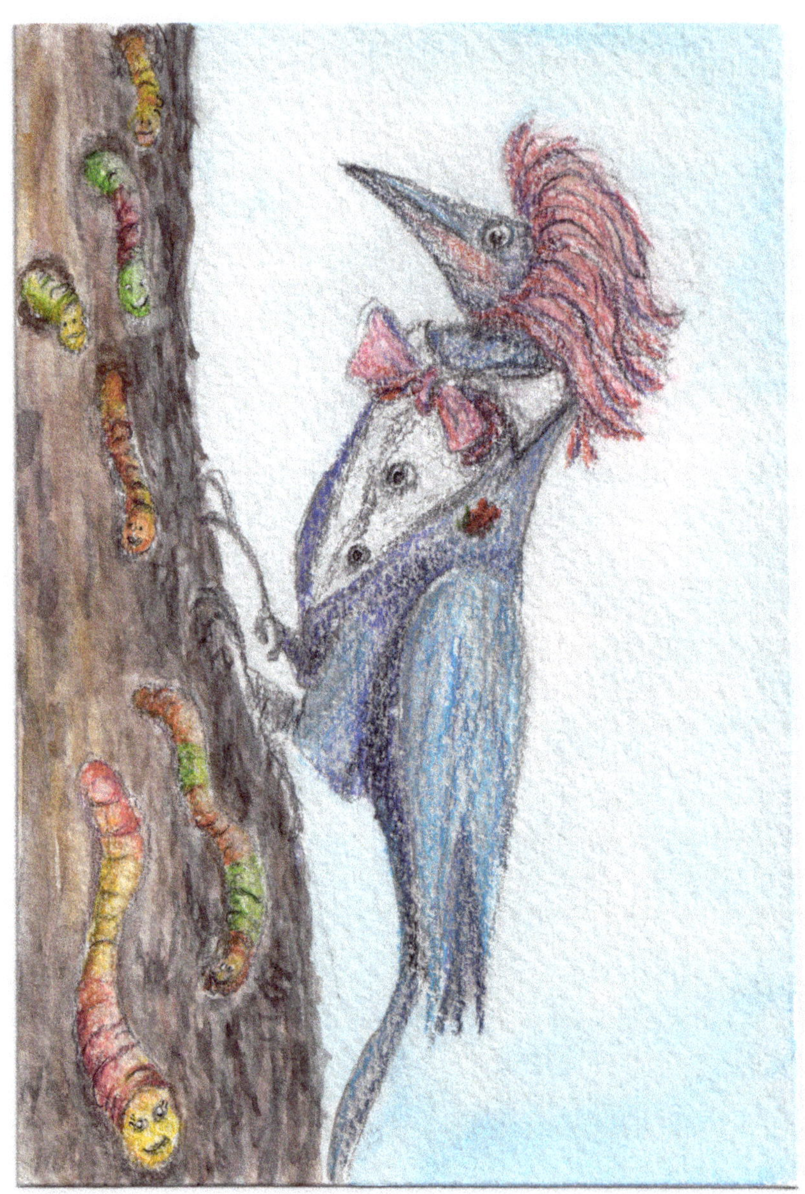

Pecking for Sweetness

Finding the sweet moments in life, when everything feels deliciously right and aligned, seems like a random game of hunt and peck these days.

Like the woodpecker, equipped since birth with the proper tools for finding food (brains that fit snugly into the skull; thick muscle in the neck to absorb impact; and a long tongue that acts as a safety belt for the brain), we too are born with a set of tools designed to assist us in partaking in the sweet nourishment of life.

While the tool forms may vary for all of us, consistent yoga and art making practices being mine, their purpose of creating connection is universal. By being present and showing up authentically in the moment, we create a space where we can tune in and connect with our true selves. Through curiosity and inquiry in these moments, we have the opportunity to engage in the act of pecking to discover who we are and the gifts we have to offer. And it is from this place of discovery we can begin to align ourselves and our lives with these unique gifts and live a life sweetened by passion and purpose.

Regrettably, somewhere along the way, the need to present ourselves in a fancy tuxedo has caused us to stray away from our true selves and the innate gifts we are here on this earth to find and share. So, remove your tuxedo and reveal your true self. Put forth the effort and make use of your innate tools. Gummy worms, the sweet moments in life, are abundant and waiting to be discovered by you and for you!

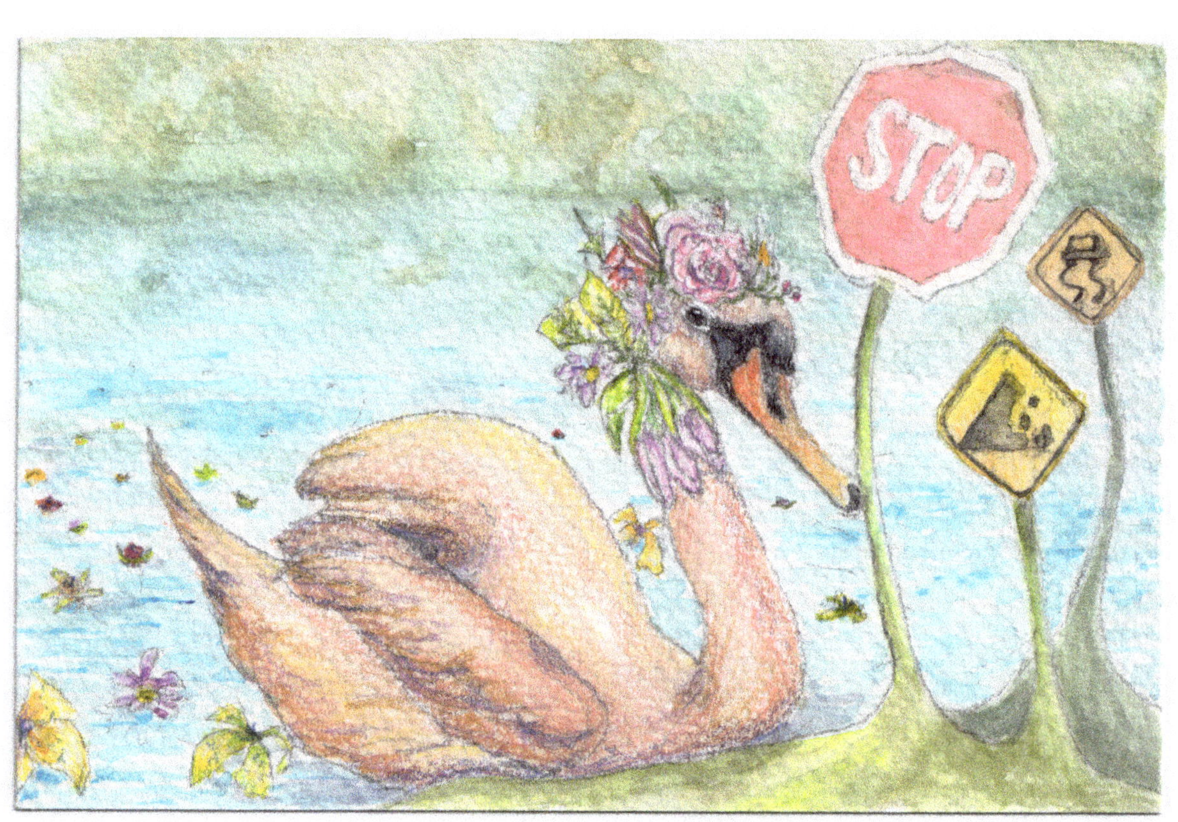
STOP

Losing My Beauty

A swan embodying the human ideals of grace and beauty glides through the water. Moving harmoniously with the natural flow of life, she gathers an array of beautiful flowers. Each blossom reflects an experience she has collected along the way of her life journey. By mid-life, the individual flowers have become a garden of radiant blossoms that she wears like a crown atop her head.

Then one day, she notices that the flowers are beginning to fall away, one by one, leaving a trail of petals behind. Glancing back, she finds herself mourning the loss of the beauty that once was hers. Looking ahead, she sees warning signs of the ego flash before her. STOP. Hold onto the flowering beauty of youth. DANGER. Slippery roads and hazardous obstacles of aging ahead. Momentarily paused by fear messages of the ego, she takes a deep breath and begins her colossal transformation.

Consciously choosing to shift the feeling of loss into a feeling of giving, she realizes for the first time in her life that the upcoming part of the journey is not about losing her flowers of experience but rather sharing them willingly with others, for each flower holds a story. A story filled with wisdom and magic that only a life lived can offer those who come after.

Looking at the floating flowers, she suddenly notices how the glistening surface of the water magnifies the colors and vibrancy of each petal. The water, full of movement and clarity, reflects the light and offers enlightenment. By transforming loss into giving, she, too, embodies the ideals of grace and beauty.

As we journey through life, we also become adorned with a crown of flowers. Which blossoms will you choose to offer up as signposts for others?

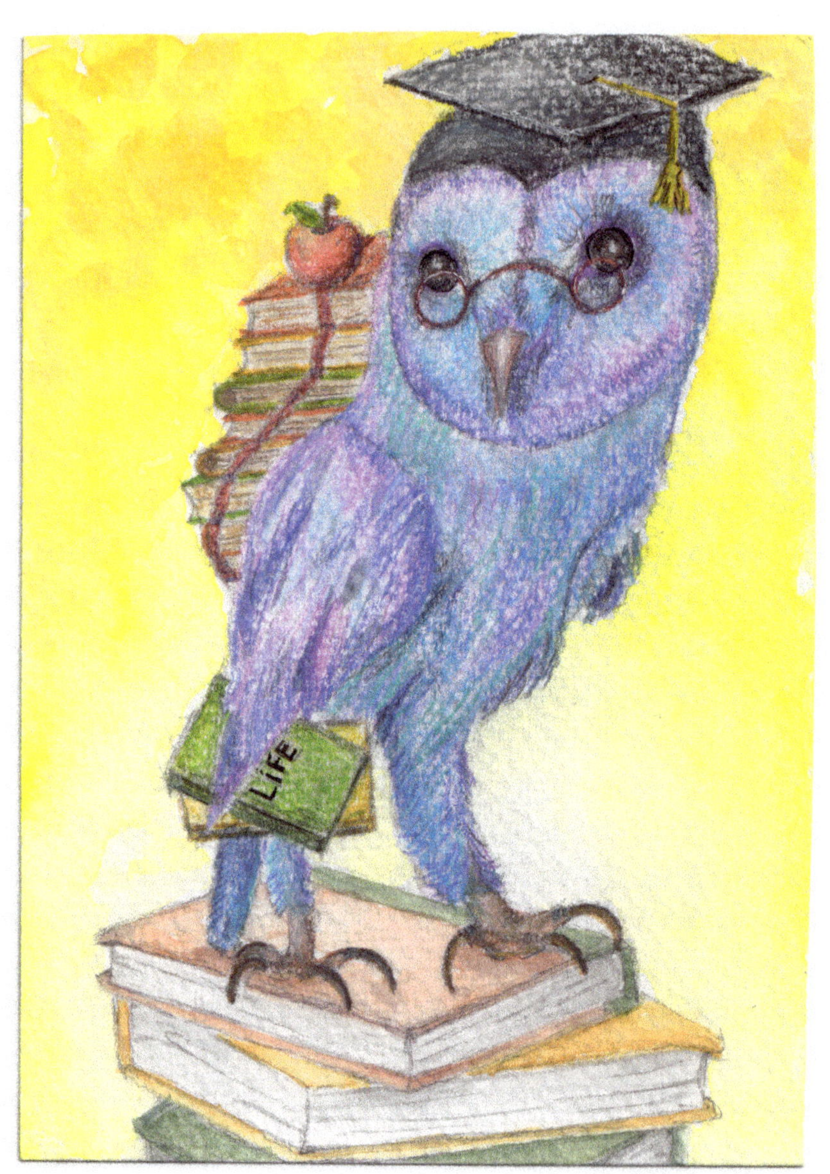

LiFE

Life Lessons

It seems these days that there are manuals for just about everything you can imagine. Just visit your favorite bookstore, and you will find topics ranging from how to repair a car to how to make friends. There are even little instruction manuals on how to live life. But no matter how much we read, research, and fill our heads with acquired knowledge, the best way to learn about life is to live it! By living mindfully, we are open to receiving and learning precisely those life lessons we are seeking answers to in books.

Being a student of life, and life-long learners, we have come to discover that the joy of learning is in the process of living the questions and not in the brief moments when we arrive at the answers. In the words of Ralph Waldo Emerson, "It's not the destination, it's the journey."

Life lessons, given to us by teachers we meet along the way, come in all forms. Those we 'like' and those we 'dislike.' Some are formal, while others are informal teachers. A teacher's lesson may be big or small. But the one thing they all have in common is that the lessons they teach are in the service of our true Self. They guide us in becoming who we are meant to be.

We will carry some lessons with us on our backs, a sort of personal reference library available to us anytime and anyplace. Others we will hold in our hands for quick reference. Sometimes the content will be so juicy that we indulge and sink our claws into them for an extended period of time. And then, there are those that serve as a high perch providing an aerial view from which we can see new perspectives and the big picture.

The truth of the world is revealed to Athena, the Greek goddess of wisdom, by an owl perched on her shoulder. Similarly, the stories we gather on our journey give us the wisdom to trust the direction our life lessons guide us. True joy and meaning in life are found not by reaching the finish line but through the gifts of experience we receive along the way!

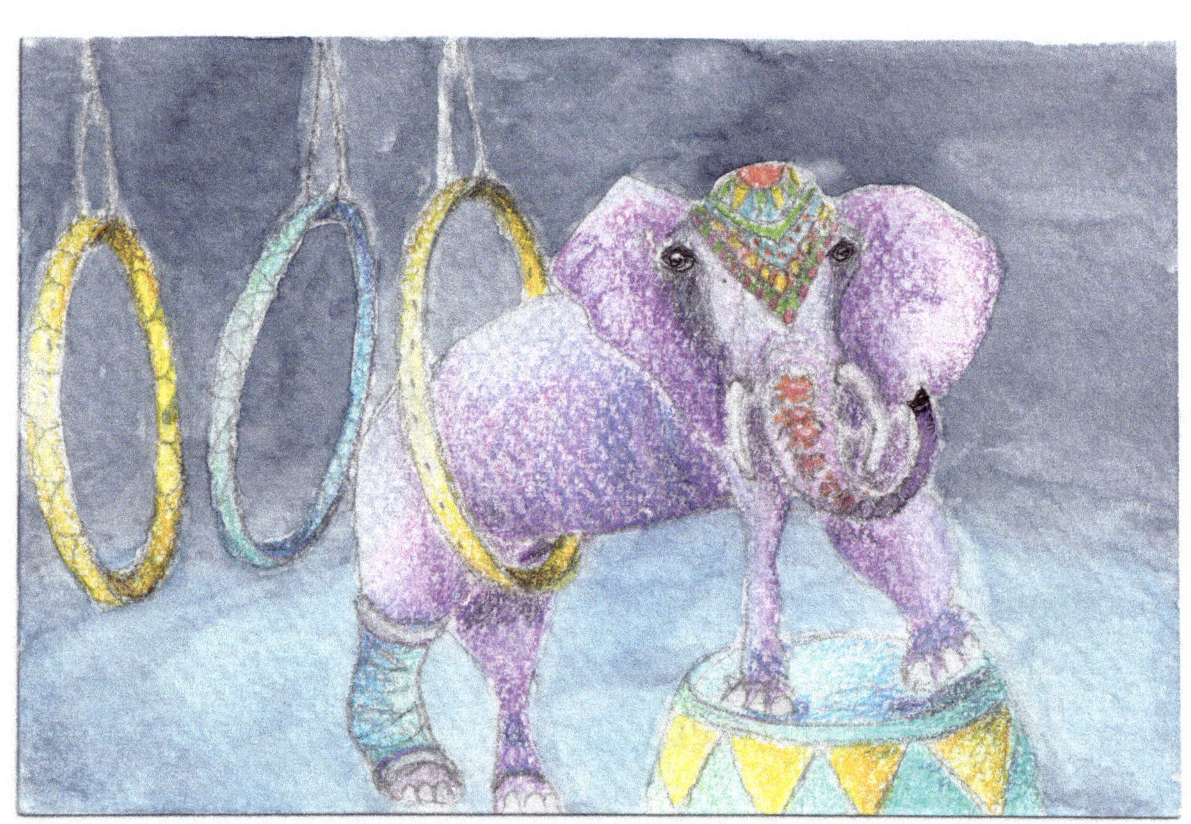

The Circus Performance

Sometimes we find ourselves showing up in our lives like an elephant performing their routine in a circus ring. The daily grind, like a circus performance, is a series of well-established and rehearsed performances. Composed of different "acts" throughout the day, the routine often becomes monotonous and mundane due to its constant repetition. In some acts, our role is to be a star performer. In some performances, we are part of the ensemble. And sometimes, we enjoy a backstage breather because the current scene excludes us completely.

The actions we perform in our headliner are learned, practiced, rehearsed, and polished to star perfection. Training sessions may be long or short, gentle or harsh, easy or challenging. The performance routines are designed to synchronize with our innate characteristics and natural abilities so that our performance appears authentic.

For our first few performances, excitement and anxiety accompany us into the ring as the novelty of being in the spotlight both thrills and frightens us. However, after several performances, it all becomes a habitual routine. We move through a sequence of steps with numbness because if we really brought awareness to the moment, we might make a mistake, slip out of character, or realize that perhaps this isn't a show we want to be in.

Sometimes our most practiced routine can have hiccups too. And although seemingly random and unpleasant, they are essential guideposts along the path of becoming our true selves. So remember, the next time something stops you in your habitual, daily routine performance, try embracing it without judgment. Welcome it with interest and curiosity. Move through the experience with gratitude, trusting that things DO happen for a reason. For they happen not TO you but rather in the service OF you!

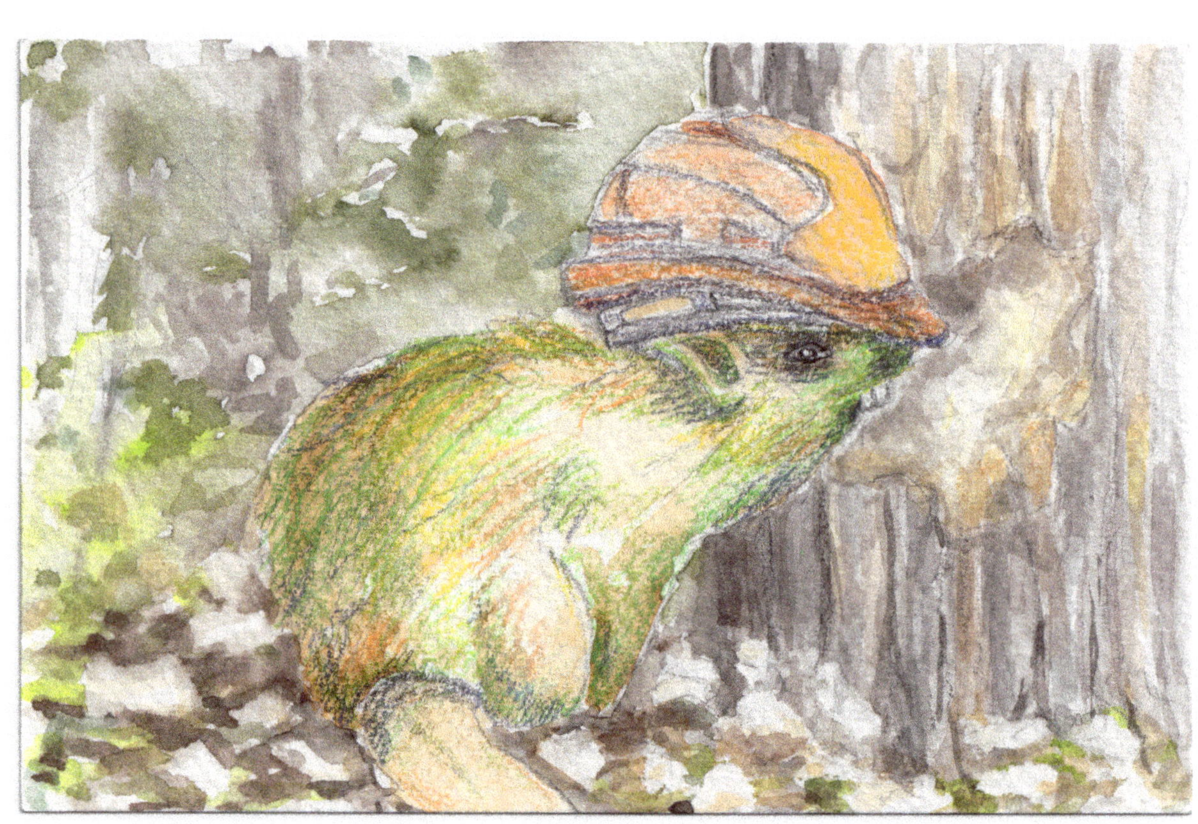

Busy as a Beaver

Ever feel like you are endlessly chomping away at a to-do list that has never been or will never be complete? Each chomp offers a brief moment of satisfaction that comes from removing an item off the list. Constantly updated and revised with lines and words, the to-do list begins to take on a life of its own, living and growing as an autonomous entity, perhaps even metamorphosing into the gatekeeper of our happiness. When we are dependent, maybe even addicted, to it as a source of satisfaction, each chomp becomes like a quick fix to satisfy our craving for doing. And thus, we begin to beautify and glorify the list because it makes us feel good.

Serving as a hard hat, the list can also assume the role of protector, warding off the overwhelm of a confusing and demanding world - both inner and outer - in the hopes of transforming chaos into order. It also offers us protection when it feels like an imminent tornado of overwhelm will cause the trees to come tumbling down on us.

While evidence of hard work is sprinkled around our feet, undeniably covering a notable percentage of ground, we ask ourselves, why is the notch, the dent of completed items barely visible on the sequoia tree-sized to-do list? Why are to-do lists seemingly never-ending? Is the to-do list a material construct of living life that, when complete, so too is our life?

Or rather, is the to-do list a never-ending notion that exists because we are alive and living life to its fullest? By finding joy in our to-do list items, we transform "have to" tasks into "get to" opportunities. The richness of life is found in the full experience of each item on the list rather than in the temporary satisfaction of crossing it off.

Do beavers experience this predicament as they work to build a dam in the natural world, or is this experience uniquely human, a side-effect of living in an artificial world?

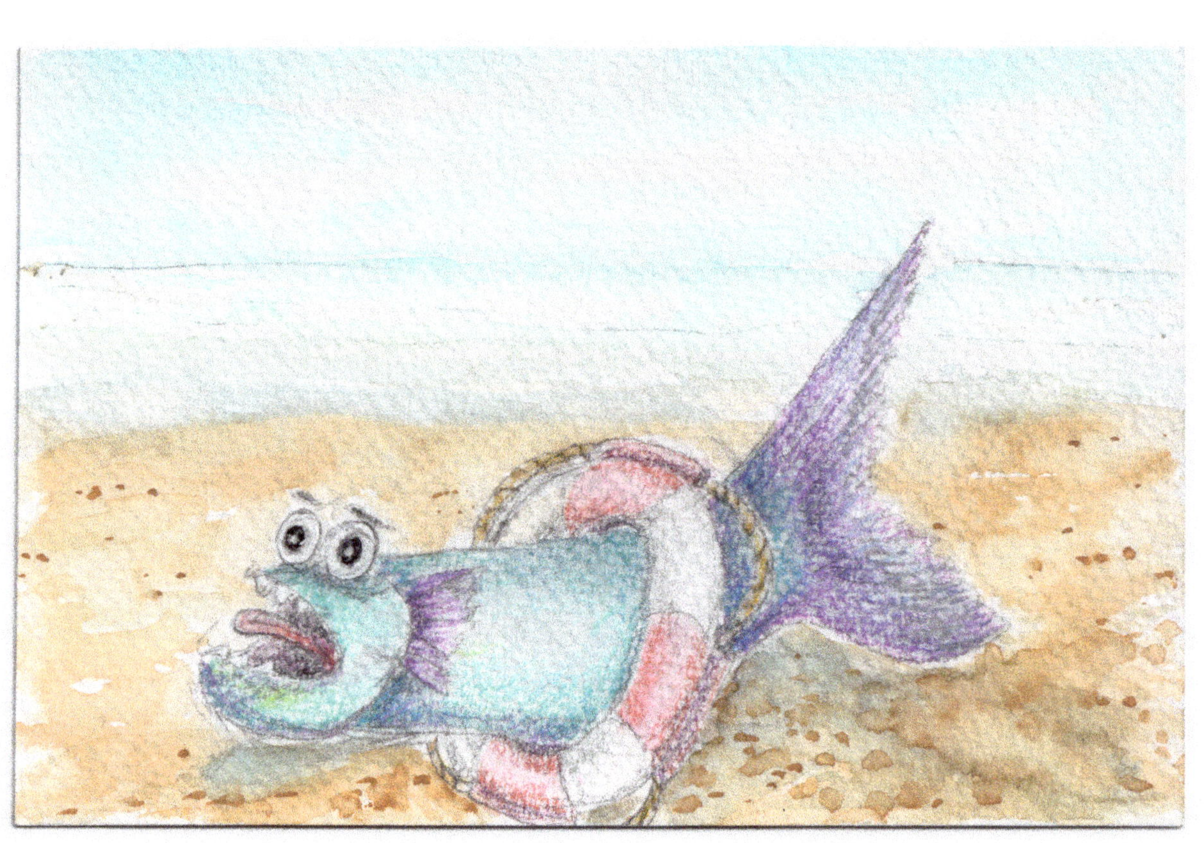

Fish Out of Water

Ever feel like you're living in someone else's story world? Experiencing a moment so far removed from what feels good and right that it feels down right out of whack? Those are the moments when our inner and outer worlds are misaligned. When we are left gasping for air, not knowing whether to fight or flee, we find ourselves feeling like a fish out of water.

In an effort to remove ourselves from a situation that we often don't even know how we got ourselves into, we flutter and flail our fins. How did the nourishing and symbiotic environment of gently caressing water that made our scales glisten and shine suddenly vanish? How did we end up on land, stuck in a life ring whose rescue function only works in water? Swaddled in a false sense of security, we find ourselves trapped by the very device designed to offer us salvation.

To begin thinking about realigning and synchronizing the inner world of our thoughts and emotions with our surroundings, we must recognize the false sense of security offered by the life ring. Then by identifying the incongruities of the two worlds, we can remove any existing obstacles and ultimately achieve salvation.

What is your false sense of security, your life ring that is making you feel like a fish out of water and holding you back from living a life in which your inner and outer worlds are aligned and coexisting in harmony?

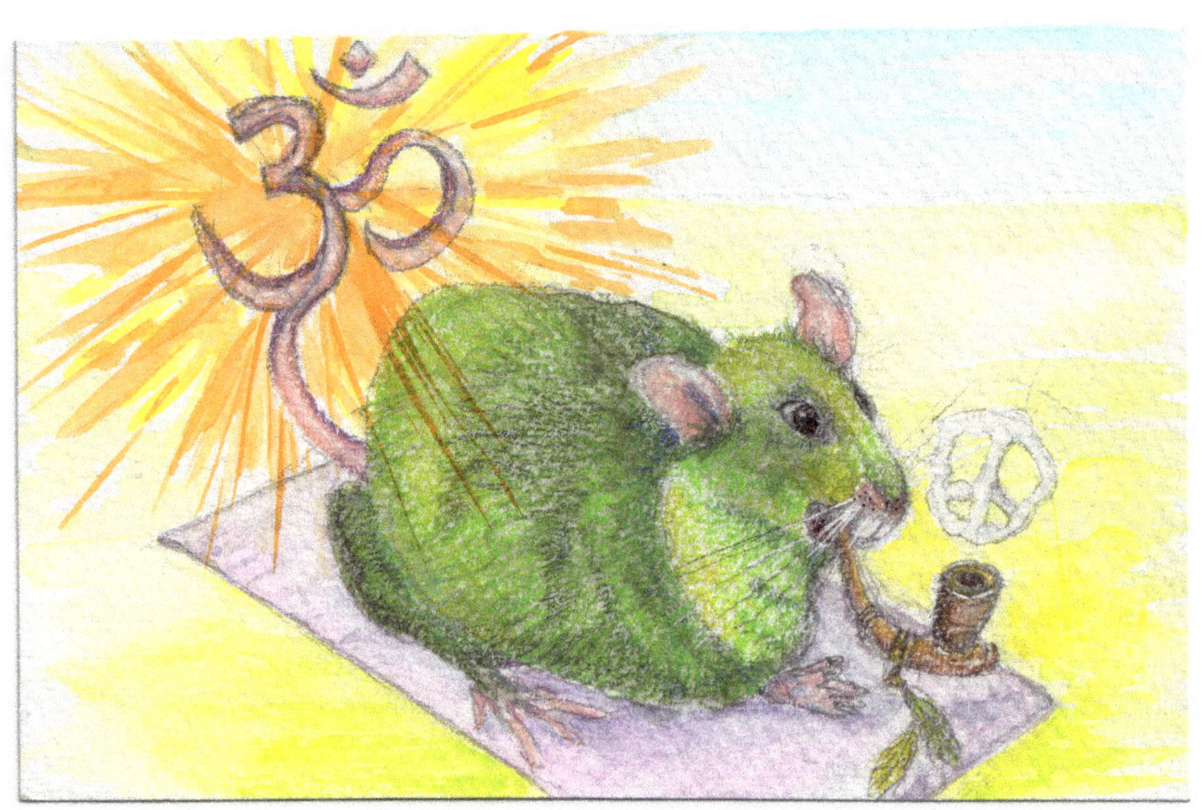

Radiate Your OM

Peace is a feeling of calmness in the mind and body that comes from deeply trusting in our heart that everything is, was, and always will be okay. There are many expressions of peace and equally as many pathways human beings use as they strive to cultivate and connect with it. Although its expression and acquisition are innumerable, we all yearn for it.

The mouse, often viewed by human beings as a carrier of disease, mirrors the feeling of dis-ease we experience. Reminding us to release the prefix 'dis' (meaning 'not') from ease, she serves as an inspiration to engage in a consistent practice that returns us to our innate state of peace.

Om, considered the sound of the universe in Indic religions, is a sacred sound that vibrates at a frequency of 432 Hz – the same vibrational frequency found in nature. By hearing and reciting the sound of Om, we harmonize the flow of energy between ourselves and nature, giving us a feeling of peace. The smoking of a peace pipe, as practiced by some cultures of Indigenous peoples, seals a treaty of peace between two disharmonized forces, as the inhalations and exhalations of breath are brought into a balanced rhythm. In yoga, an asana is a steady and comfortable position. Through the sequencing of asanas in a yoga practice, we create a flow that re-members and realigns our dis-membered, disconnected body, mind, breath, and soul.

Our practice is a personal portal into a world of peace. The appearance of our practice is not important as it is often impermanent and changing throughout our lives. What is important, however, is that we have at least one go-to tool in our box that gives us access to a world of peace anytime and anywhere. For it is in this sacred space that we retreat and rejuvenate as we tap into the omnipresent well of peace. Only when we replenish ourselves can we truly experience peace and radiate it authentically into the world.

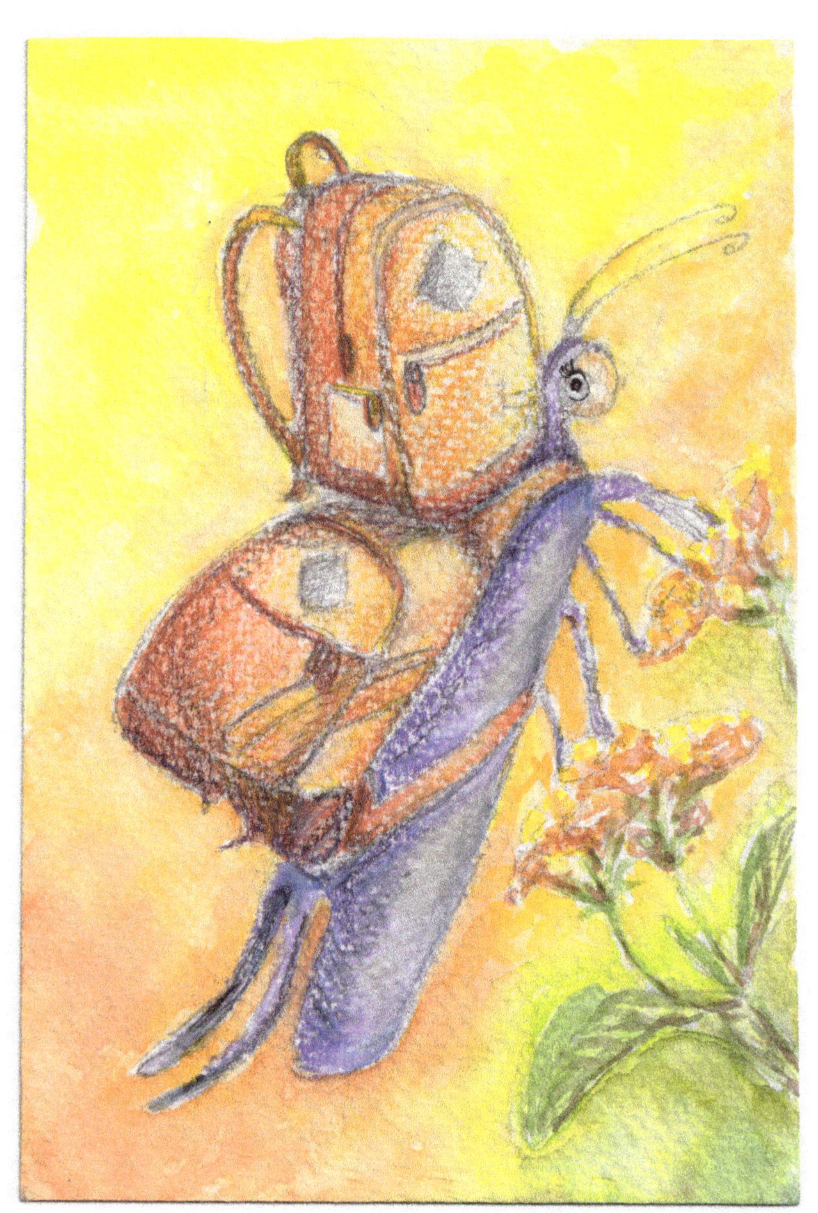

I Can Fly

Butterflies develop the strength to break through their cocoon by effortfully batting their wings against the inner walls of the chrysalis. This process releases a chemical that strengthens wing muscles enabling butterflies to break through and fly to freedom. This essential, albeit painful, experience is a critical step in the development of a butterfly.

In addition to serving an essential function, a butterfly's wings are their most beautiful, colorful, and adored characteristic. They are the element by which we recognize and identify individual species. Strong and vibrant at birth, the once beautiful and uplifting wings become damaged and tattered as they go through life. Like the butterfly, throughout our lives, we become weighted down by the burdens we accumulate. Until one day, we realize our wings, that used to lift us, have transformed into backpacks, and we have lost our ability to fly.

Like the caterpillar whose transformation occurs in the safety of a chrysalis, we need to give ourselves the time to go inward and examine the contents of our backpacks. This evaluation process is an opportunity to transform limiting burdens and confinement into uplifting freedom. Keep in the pack what fits and let go of the rest. Like butterflies, we were born to fly light and free, spreading beauty and pollinating the world with joy and love.

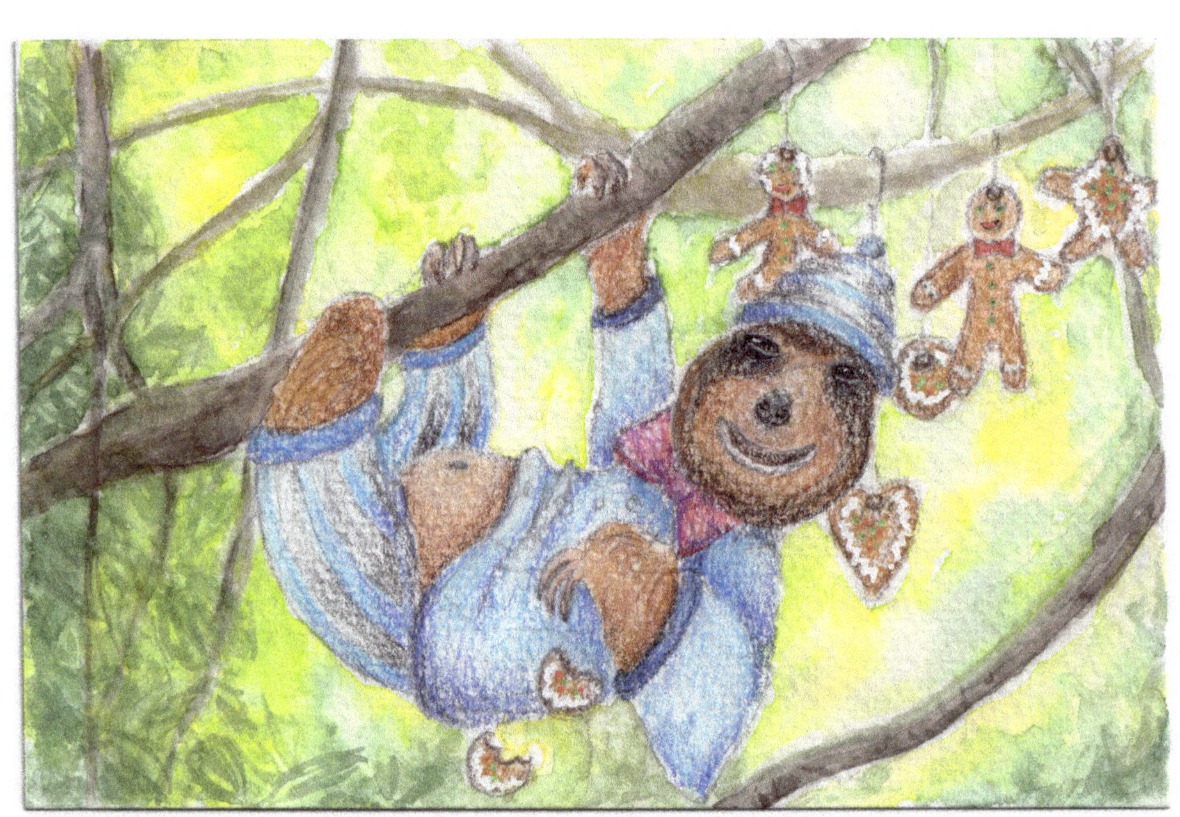

Overstuffed

We have all experienced the feeling of overeating. Ingesting too much of something, albeit good, at least once in our life. That moment when having a second, third, or even fourth serving lands us in comatose dreamlike slumber. Surrendering to this state, we find ourselves saying I wish I hadn't or if only I could, rather than accepting ourselves and the moment as it is.

Filling ourselves to the point of overstuffing can compensate for the feeling of scarcity. A belief in not being or not having enough that we are attempting to fill. An intangible hunger of inadequacy that we are trying to satiate. But what do we do when we discover this hunger, our deep-rooted feeling of scarcity, is insatiable? Realizing that no amount of cookies, money, and material goods will ever be able to fill the physical void, we shift our focus to the invisible, energetic realm of our emotional body.

What we choose to overeat in the external world can provide clues about the ways in which we are starving in our inner worlds. Is it food, material goods, people, or knowledge we are craving? The proverbial saying "you are what you eat" reminds us that this uncomfortable, overstuffed moment is actually an opportunity. A gift in the form of a window through which we get a peek into our mind. And it is there, in the habitat of our thoughts, that we see a landscape filled with entwined leaves and vines. And we recognize that these temping, leafy greens are the fluctuations of our minds.

Like a sloth who hangs upside-down to better reach the fresh and, therefore, less toxic leaves, we also need to invert our position. We need to see our hunger from a different perspective to reduce the amount of toxins we habitually consume. By slowing down to a sloth-like pace, we bring awareness to the fluctuations of the mind. By mindfully choosing how we nourish ourselves and taking in each leaf individually, we give ourselves a chance to see beyond the entwined vines and leaves of our thoughts. And with each slowly ingested leaf, the openings in the cluster expand to reveal a shining light, the source and nourishment of our truly abundant and fruitful inner landscape. We have always had and always will have all that we are and need!

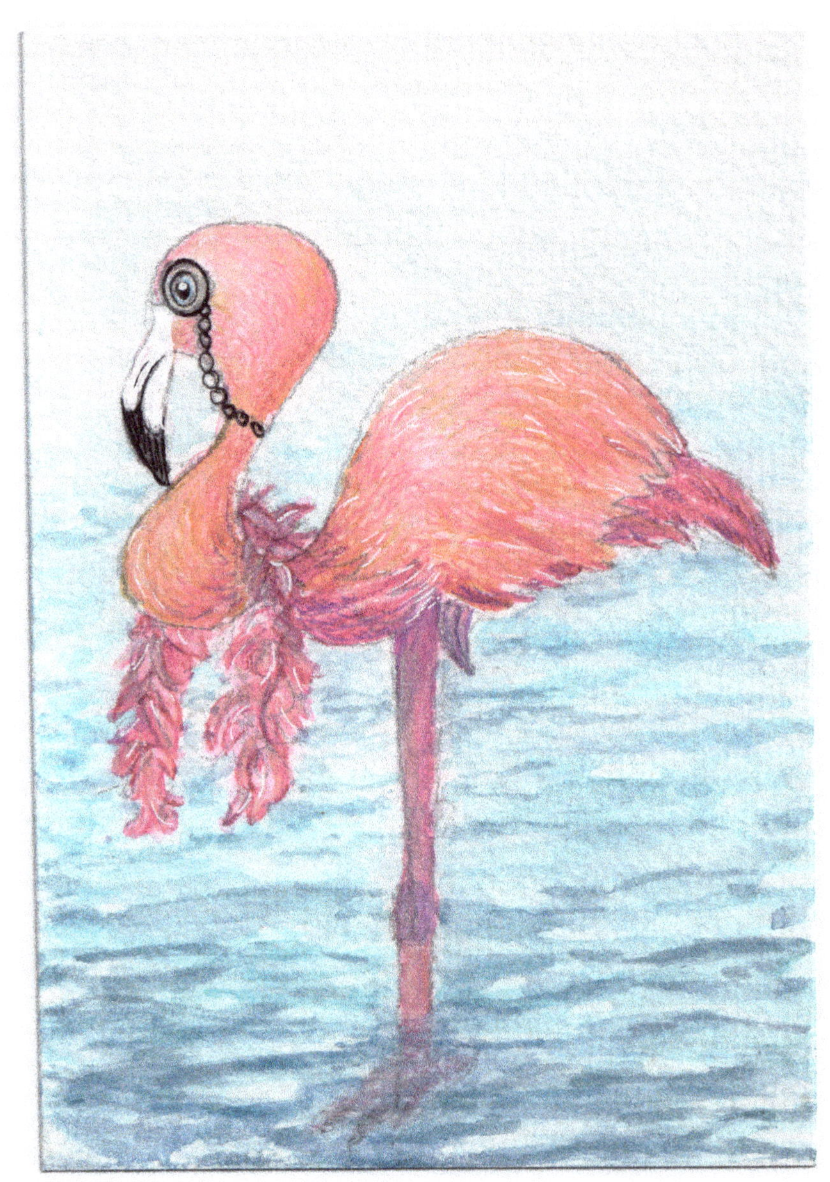

Balancing with Monocle

The monocle is a type of corrective lens that is designed to enhance visual perception in one eye. The flamingo increases his stability and longevity by implementing the energy-saving mode of standing on one leg. Modern day cell phones have an energy-efficient function that can be activated by the touch of a finger. But what about us? How do we tap into our energy reserves and maximize our efficiency?

By reconnecting with our true selves, we discover that we also have inherent energy reserves. The flamingo, using a monocle to improve his vision, reminds us that we find our inner balance by spending time alone, standing solo. Taking the time to connect with our feelings and thoughts, permitting ourselves to be, we tap into the strength and stability found in standing forthright, unapologetically, and authentically in this world.

So wrap yourself in the fanciest boa and celebrate the beauty that is YOU! Stand, shine, and show off your glorious Self. What are the tools that lead you back to yourself? Define, embrace, and use them regularly, for there is a strong and energized YOU yearning to shine and be seen. Only by tuning in with your magnificent YOUness and feeling true inner balance can you be aligned and in harmony with yourself, others, and the world!

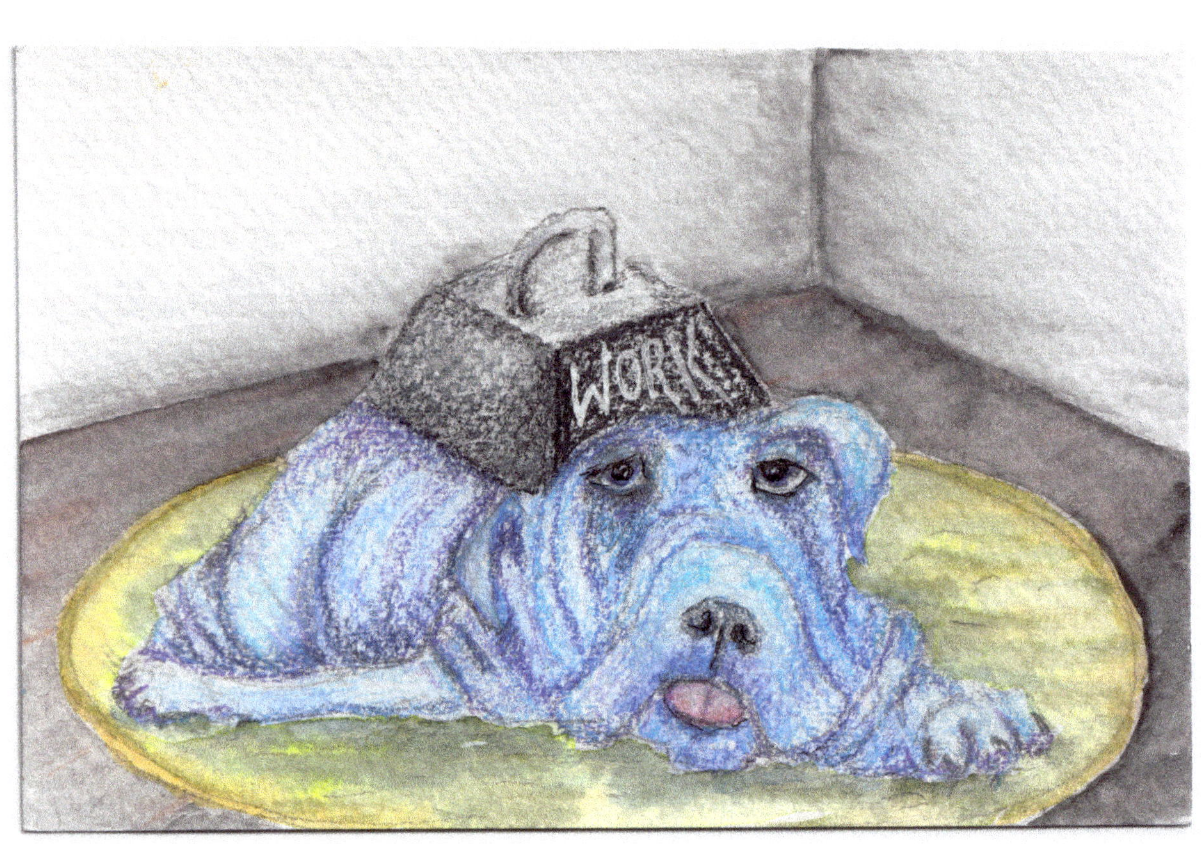

WORK

Dog Tired

A healthy work-life balance means giving equal weight to the work and personal aspects of our lives. But how do we achieve balance when feeling dog tired and too exhausted to move? What do we do when the weight of work is so heavy, causing us to get stuck underneath? Compressed with overwhelm and fatigue, our vision begins to blur, and we become blind to possibility. Losing sight of those weights that once nourished and rejuvenated us, we lose the counter-balance they offer and find ourselves settling into a feeling of helplessness and perhaps even hopelessness. What do we do then?

The mass scales used thousands of years ago are a reminder that sometimes a variety of weights are needed to achieve balance. Furthermore, these weights need to be continually evaluated and adjusted in order to maintain balance over time. However, unlike the old-fashioned mass scales, which are designed to have a static equilibrium, life is not static.

The key to achieving a work-life balance is not to strive towards the maintenance of a static balance but rather the recognition that there will be moments in life that tip the scales in one direction or the other, and it is this movement that releases stuckness and induces flow. Does it have to be an either-or? Must two sides of a scale work as opposing forces against each other rather than in a harmonious up and down? Envision instead the graceful movement of a teetering seesaw giving and receiving with effort and ease. An equal exchange of working and playing that is constantly shifting and changing form.

Letting go of the need to attain a fixed work-life balance releases rigidity and control. We no longer feel the need to forcefully grip and hold in place the weights for fear of getting 'stuck' underneath one of them. True internal equilibrium comes from the comfort of knowing and trusting that the disbalance we feel in a given moment is not permanent but rather a temporary, fleeting experience. To be in movement is to be alive, and is living not the essential component of both the work and the personal aspects of one's life?

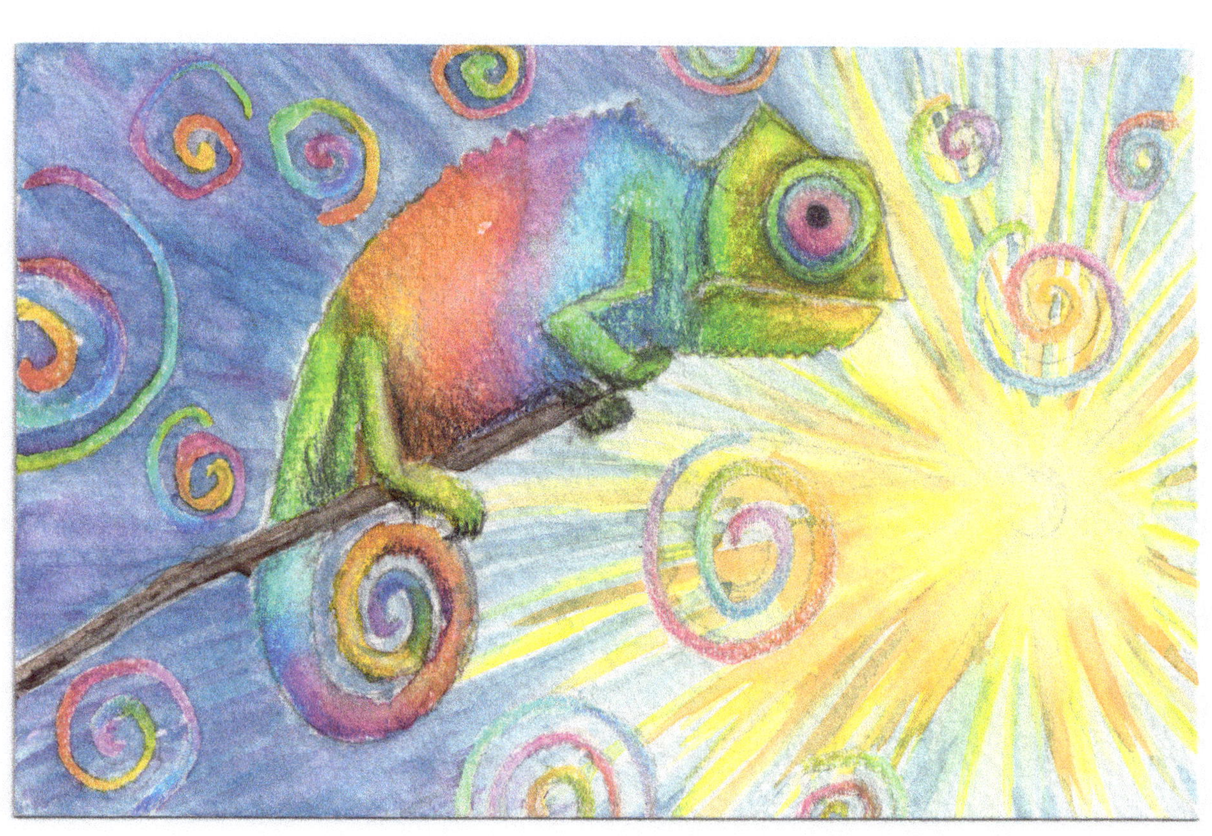

Camouflage Breakthrough

The chameleon changes color with the intention of camouflaging, blending into the environment, for the purpose of concealment. This form of social signaling takes place in the presence of another being and is determined by a chameleon's physiological condition and intention. As humans, we also learn to change the colors of who we are to adapt and fit in with our environments. By camouflaging ourselves, we avoid standing out as different from those around us in an attempt to hide our feelings of discomfort, self-consciousness, and anxiety triggered by being out of place.

Sometimes color change is necessary to keep us safe. However, often it actually poses a threat to our identity. If habitually done, the transformation of camouflaging becomes a subconscious action, and we risk extinguishing what we are desperately trying to protect. Overdone, the perceived safety of being invisible causes destruction or even complete elimination of who we are. Because by taking on multiple colors and identities, we forget our original color and become invisible even to ourselves.

Imagine yourself in an environment where only a few or none of your colors are reflected in the surroundings. What would happen if, instead of concealing your colors to blend in, you set them free, allowing them to burst and radiate like a magical spectacular fireworks show? And as the colors swirled through the air, the world, like a blank canvas, embraced your unique hues as invaluable elements of the emerging artwork.

No longer living under the protective guise of camouflage, the true beauty of who you are, the gifts you have to offer, and the real reason you are here become visible for all the world to see. So, what are you waiting for? Break through your camouflage, stand out, and shine, for the time is NOW!

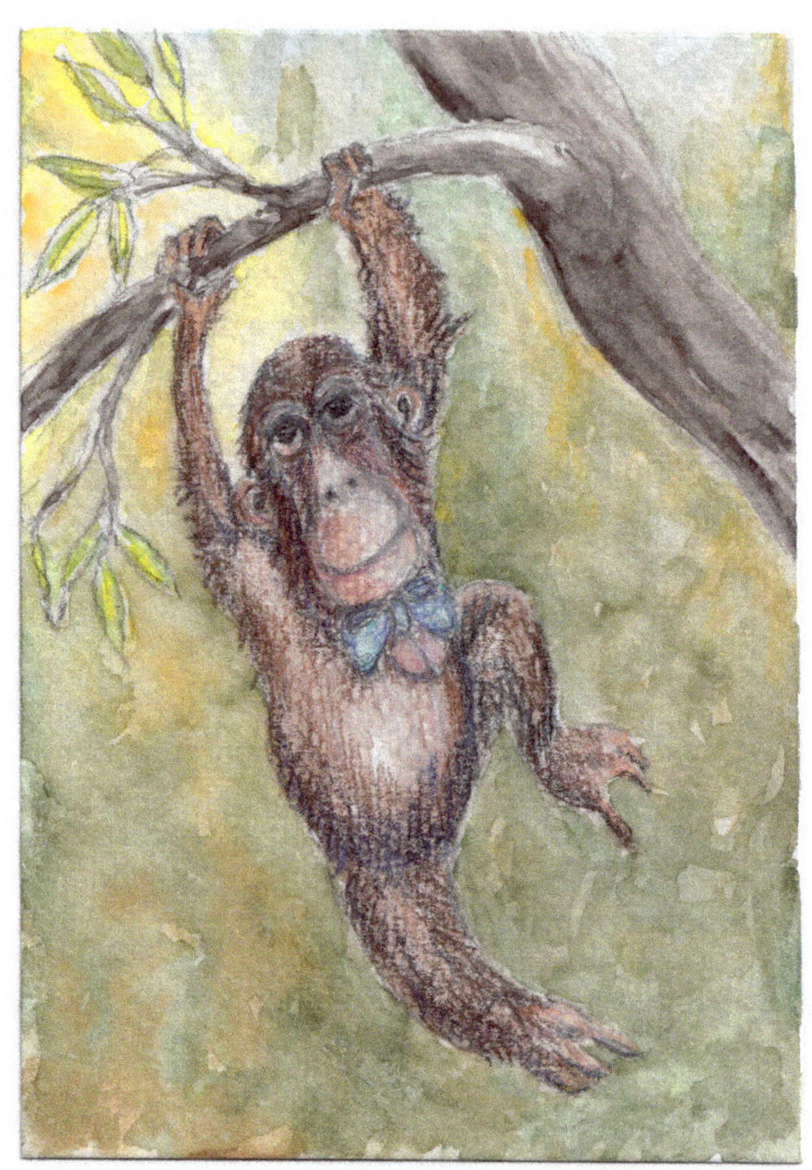

Dangling in a Monkey Suit

There are times in our life when we find ourselves dressed in what feels like a monkey suit, a type of uniform to fit our role. This suit partially reflects who we are, after all, we share 98.8% of our DNA with chimpanzee monkeys. The other part, however, feels so foreign to us that not only do we feel uncomfortable in it, but we also don't even recognize ourselves while wearing it.

We are born wearing a birthday suit. Until we leave this world, we are given a full wardrobe of suits from which to choose. Throughout our life, we try on different ones. Some will fit as if they were made for us. Some may need to be tailored just a bit to obtain the perfect fit. And some will downright not fit us at all for a variety of reasons. Sometimes our suits, like that favorite t-shirt ridden with holes, will accompany us for what seems like a lifetime, while others will last but a brief night out. Some pieces will be hand-me-downs, gifts, or personally purchased pieces. And although we will outgrow most of them at some point in our life, we find our favorite only by trying them all on.

But what do you do if you find yourself dangling in a suit that doesn't fit or feel right? Yet, you know that if you use your hands to try and remove it, you will be forced to 'let go' of the very branch you are clutching onto so tightly for comfort and security? Would you choose to live out your life in the discomfort of an ill-fitting suit, or would you risk letting go in order to find a suit that really suits you?

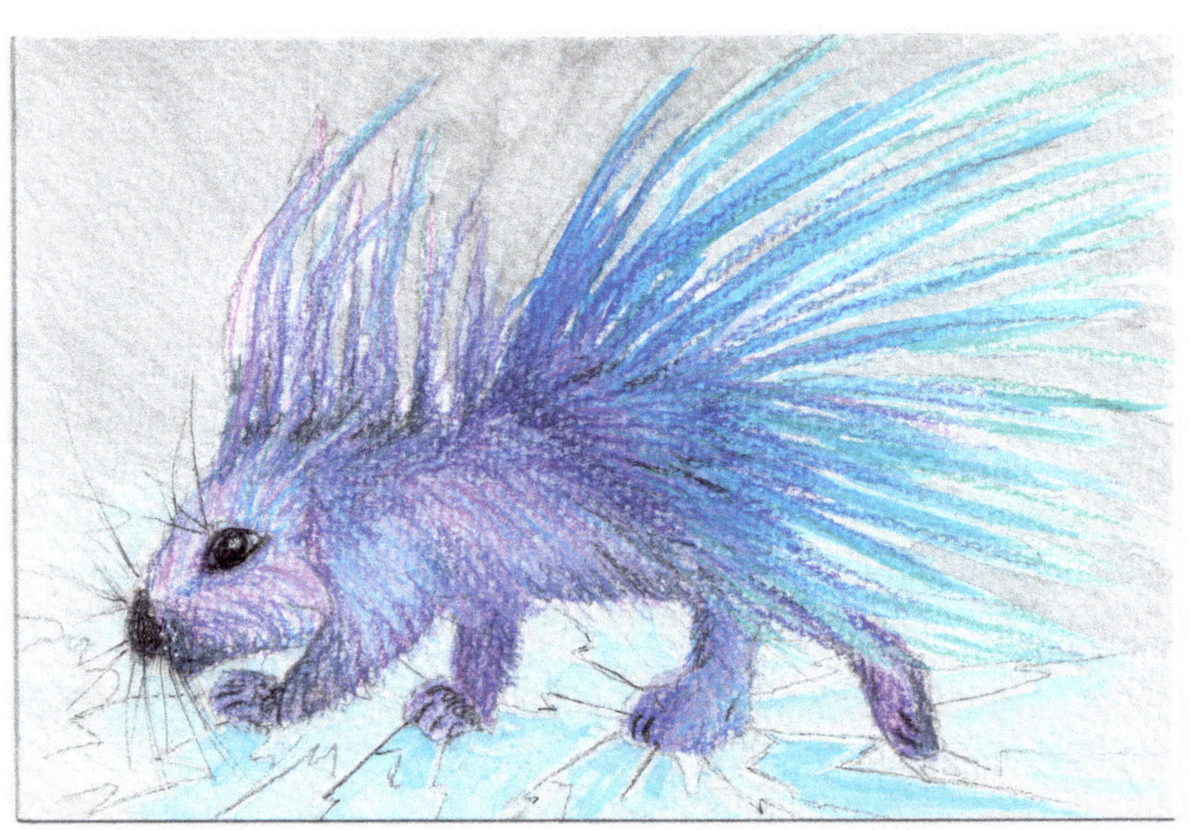

Feeling Prickly

Showing our prickly side can sometimes feel like we are "walking on thin ice." We are taking a risk that may have unpleasant and sometimes serious consequences. Expressing negative feelings is often perceived by others as something uncomfortable and undesirable. As a result, we punish ourselves for feeling this way and label ourselves as being bad. But just like the quills of porcupines are inherently part of their identity and contribute to their beauty, so do our feelings. They are part of who we are and make us whole and beautiful.

Porcupines use their quills as a tangible form of communication for intangible feelings. Quill activation is an expression of fear and serves as a warning sign for potential predators. Like the porcupine, we have quills that express our emotions and are a warning signal for others. Tears of rage, tantrums of frustration, and the silence of sadness are just a few examples of how we express and release what words cannot. A language of emotion that we have developed and used since we took our first breath.

Expressing our feelings makes us vulnerable, so it feels like we are "walking on thin ice". However, sharing the entire spectrum of our emotions is an essential component of the human experience. No matter how thin the ice may feel, the weight of unreleased emotions will inevitably accumulate and ultimately cause us to break through the surface of the ice.

Therefore, next time you feel prickly and find yourself debating whether or not you should risk emotional expression, remember that walking on thin ice is better than breaking and crashing through it.

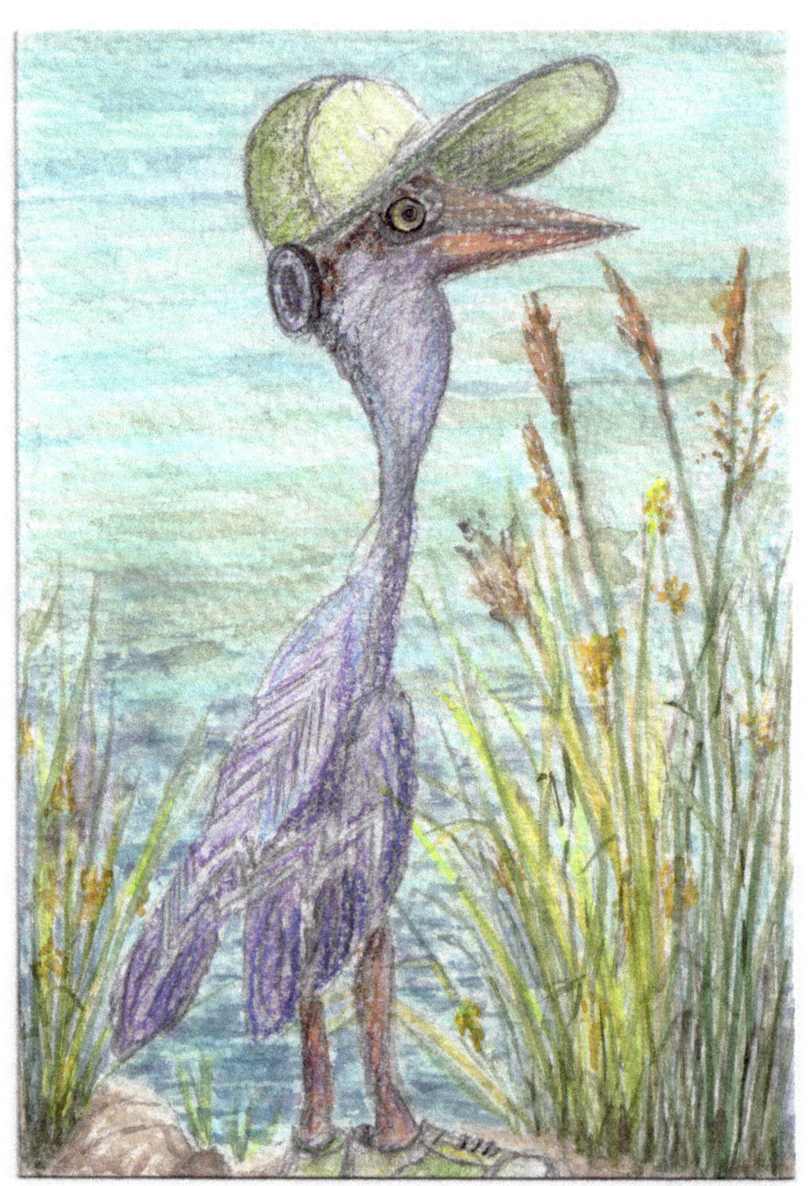

Running Randy

Life gives us many opportunities to run. Sometimes we run to catch something, while other times, we run to flee. The best run, however, is the one that takes you back to yourself and returns you to a natural flow state of being. One that reconnects you with the inhalations and exhalations of your breath to remind you of all that inspires you and everything that needs to be released.

The onset of a run gets our gears moving. As we persevere, the initial grinding and screeching feeling of our body's rusty cogs diminishes, and we realize that motion is lotion. With every stride, we get more in sync as the initial bumpy and clumsy rotations are transformed into smooth, well-oiled gears. Similarly, our thoughts, previously disjointed, overwhelming, and stuck, slowly begin to loosen and shift. A feeling of clarity emerges, a sense of lightness and ease, with which our thoughts and bodies move. No longer spinning viscously out of control in our heads, thoughts find their place.

The running movement, a consistent rhythm of inhaling and exhaling, synchronizes our flow and our alignment with the energy of the universe. And through this calibration, we realize how supported we are by a loving universe. This feeling gives us the strength and courage to fly with a lightness of being and a sense of freedom. We experience our ability to reach heights greater than we initially felt possible when the rusty, grinding cogs weighed us down.

Like Randy the heron, once we are flying in sync with universal flow, we too embody the grace and serenity characteristic of this majestic bird. As he waits, believing the next catch will come, we begin to trust that everything we need will be given to us when the time is right. For the universe will always provide for us. We just need to trust it!

In the space of calmness and clarity created by the flow of our breath, we return to our heart center. Here we connect with trust, the truth of our journey, that serves as a reminder of why we are here. It is no coincidence that our biggest 'aha' moments are experienced on a run, and we think, Yes, that's it!

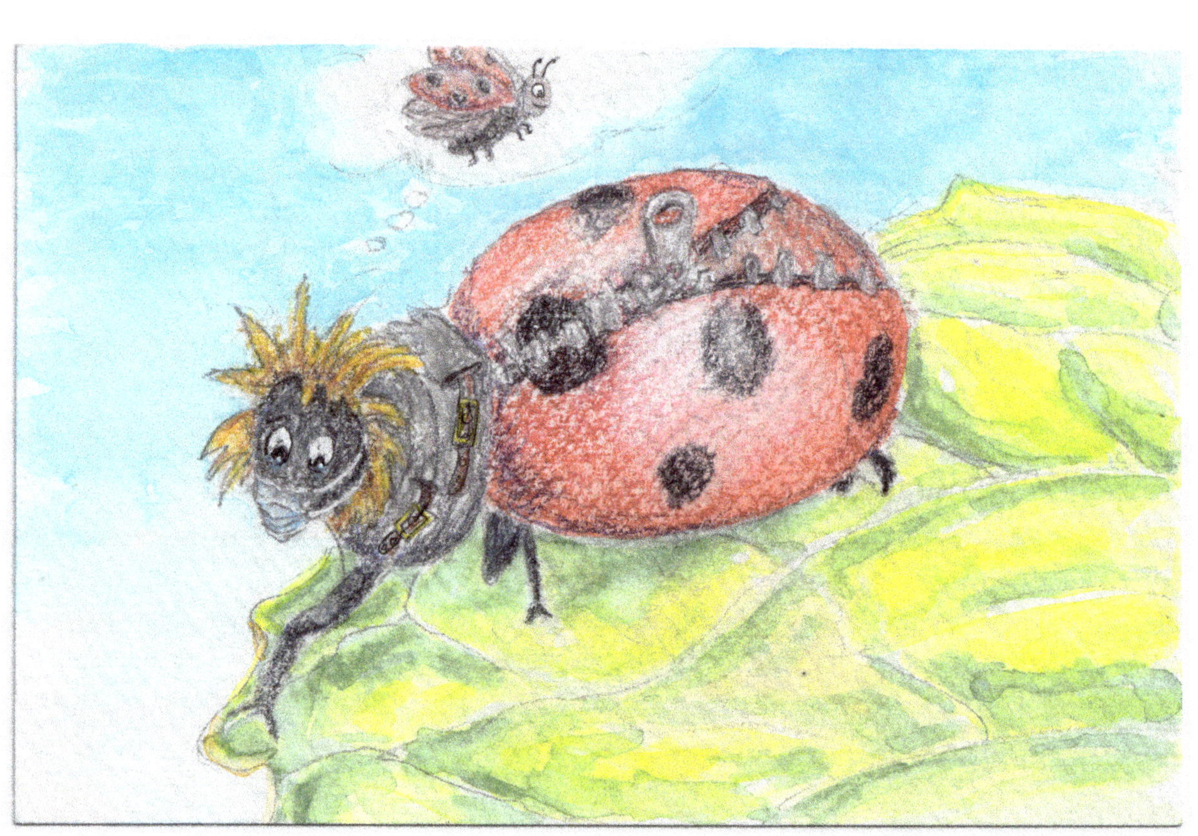

The Daily Grind

On the first day of vacation, wings charged with freedom and vitality, the ladybug sits on top of a green leaf aglow with sunshine, feeling like the luckiest creature alive! Albeit exhausted from the long and tiresome journey to arrive at this moment, the limitless potential of an upcoming holiday fills her with unbound energy. It's a time to simply be and reconnect with the essence of her ladybugness. The past months have left her feeling lost in the role of being someone else, performing to appease and fulfill the expectations of daily work and life routines.

It is within the space of vacation that the essence, the spirit of who a ladybug is, can be replenished. Yet, in the blink of an eye, days diminish, and the ladybug begins to feel the zipper of the daily grind closing, one tooth at a time, limiting the freedom of her wings. And as the buckles of the straight jacket are pulled tighter and tighter, the ability of her hands to create is restricted. The mask, reinstated under the guise of protection, feels more like suffocation, a stifling of the breath that earlier had filled her wings with optimism and excitement.

Thoughts of how am I going to survive this begin spinning in her head. A feeling she knows will continue until the next hopeful moment of vacation once again removes the binds and frees her from the daily grind. And so the cycle continues, year after year.

Yet the ladybug, knowing hope is an optimistic state of mind, realizes she can never be truly zipped, tied, or masked.

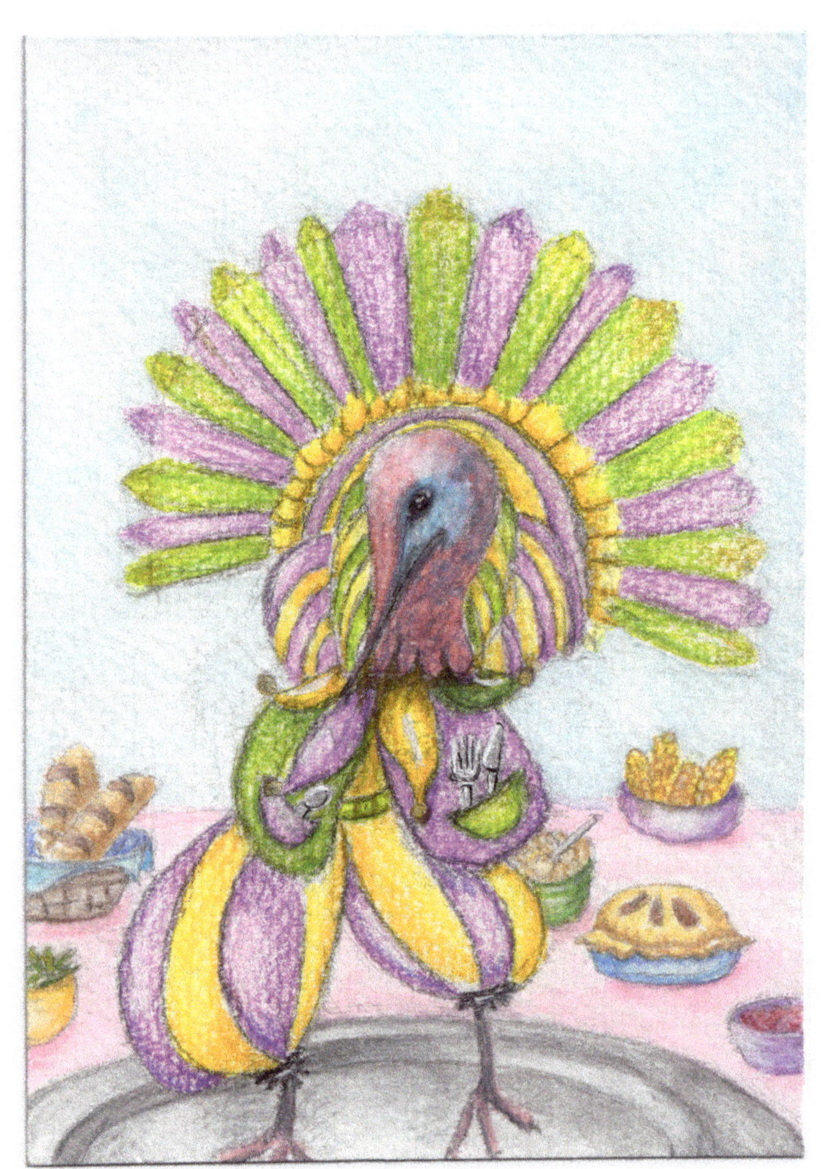

The Turkey Jester

Thanksgiving, a day of giving thanks, although rooted in religious and cultural traditions around the world, is perhaps the most widely celebrated national and secular holiday in the United States.

The turkey is the star of the Thanksgiving show - a celebrity around whom fixings, family, friends, and football fans congregate. Only to be cooked and eaten by the very spectators who adore him. Does the turkey, summoned before his fans, assume the role of a jester for our Thanksgiving court? A jester, defined as a person who habitually plays the fool, entertains the council and household of a king's court.

Arriving at the annual Thanksgiving dinner dressed in the finest, brightly colored attire, armed with exquisitely polished silverware in his jacket pockets, the turkey jester is prepared to join the feast as an itinerant performer and food. Is the fate of landing on the dinner platter unbeknownst to the turkey, or is it fulfilling the assigned role of court jester and playing the fool?

Imagine, one Thanksgiving Day, giving thanks in the form of a turkey pardon, extending an invitation to the turkey to join the table as an honorary guest alongside fixings, family, friends, and football fans. Celebrating together as equal fellow beings. Would that not be the quintessence of giving thanks?

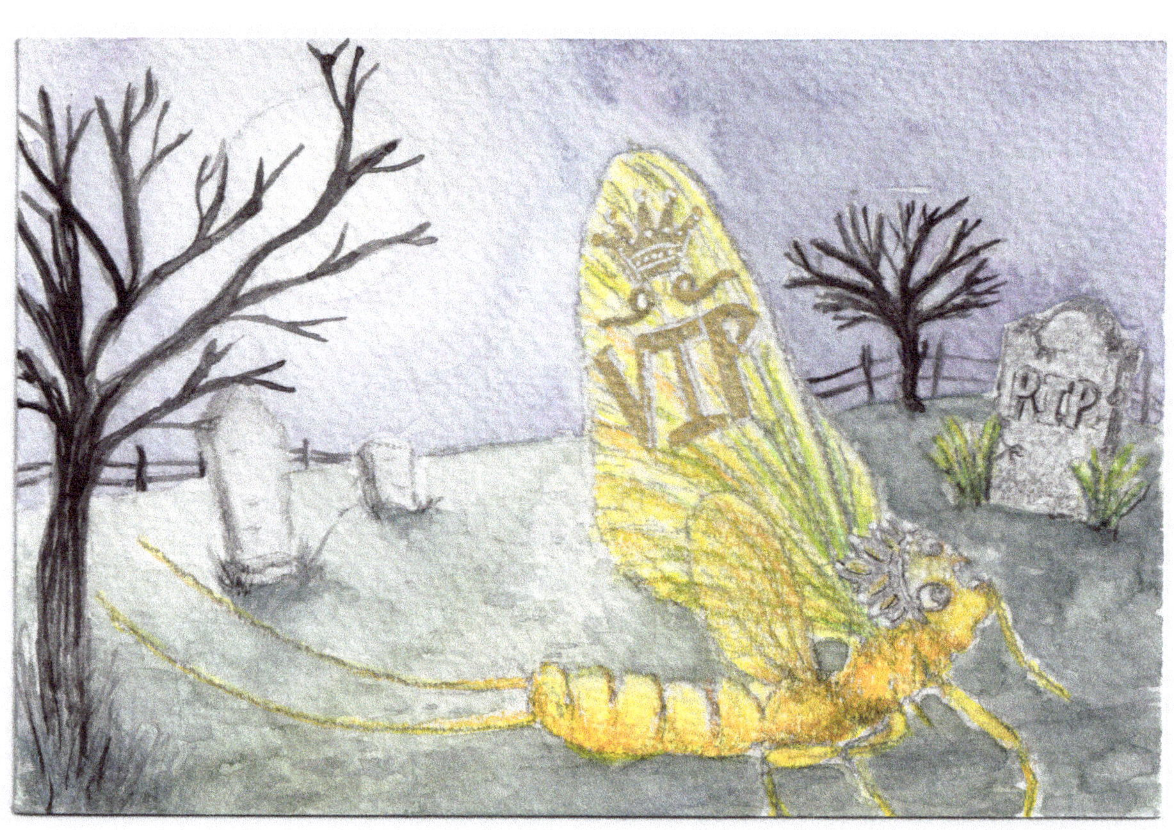

The Freedom of Unimportance

The German word for mayfly is 'Eintagsfliege.' Translated, 'Eintagsfliege' is 'One Day Fly' because they have a lifespan of only twenty-four hours. Compared with the 700,800 hours of an average human lifespan (80 years) gifted to us at birth, a life consisting of twenty-four hours seems comparatively unimportant. But frankly, what determines insignificance in this comparison, and is being unimportant truly a negative as the prefix 'un' (meaning 'not') suggests?

By cloaking ourselves with a cape of humbleness, a veil of invisibility for the ego, we can transform the feeling of unimportance into a feeling of freedom. Freedom from pressure to perform, please, and live in misalignment with our authentic Selves. While striving for VIP status, the recognition, the affirmation, and the self-confidence it superficially provides, we will ultimately be steered to RIP status, dying from not being seen, loved, and trusted for who we truly are.

So, the next time you feel unimportant, picture a mayfly, seemingly minute in space and time, flying through the air. Notice the lightness of being that characterizes this creature's brief lifespan, and say to yourself, "I may feel unimportant, but I am FREE!"

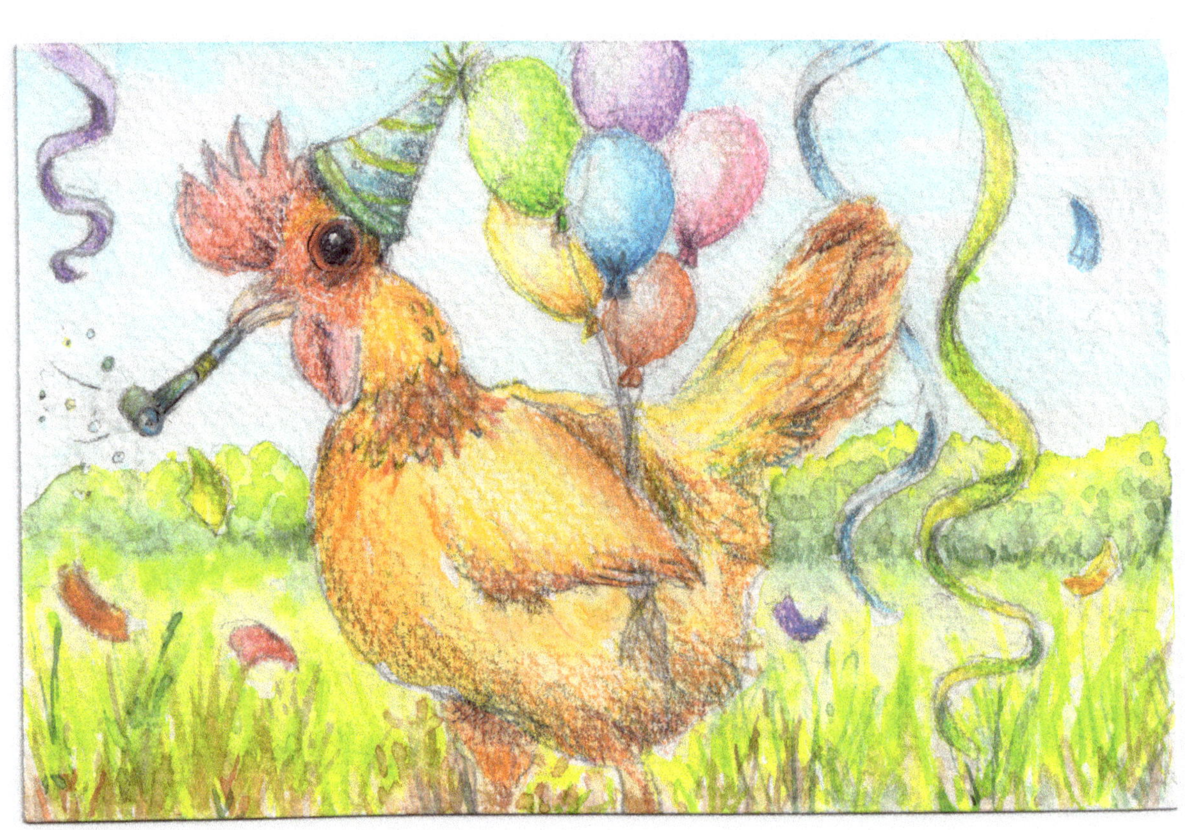

Did They Have a Good Life?

The key to living a harmonious, peaceful, no-regrets life is engaging in mindful interactions with all beings. Too often, we create and apply criteria with which we categorize and ultimately label another being as worthy or worthless. And by doing so, we create an otherness, a detached space of ignorance, into which we can pour discrimination.

Beginning with the chicken on your plate, before you mindlessly dig in, ask yourself, "did they have a good life?" Taking this moment to acknowledge your commonality negates the blinding effects of judgment. Seeing similarities and feeling gratitude for the shared experience, we act in a manner free of regret and aligned with the heart, mind, and body.

Extending this compassion to the interactions beyond the plate to all beings we encounter anytime and anywhere facilitates a life of harmony. A life where we are at peace with ourselves, each other, and the world. A life that is regret-free, no longer dividing and expending our energy on futile looking back filled with guilt and remorse. Rather, we are free to give all our energy to what is happening in the present.

A mindful moment in the presence of another being, focused on what I can do right here and right now, to make sure I make my contribution to this being's life. So that they, too, at the end of their time, are able to say, "I had a good life."

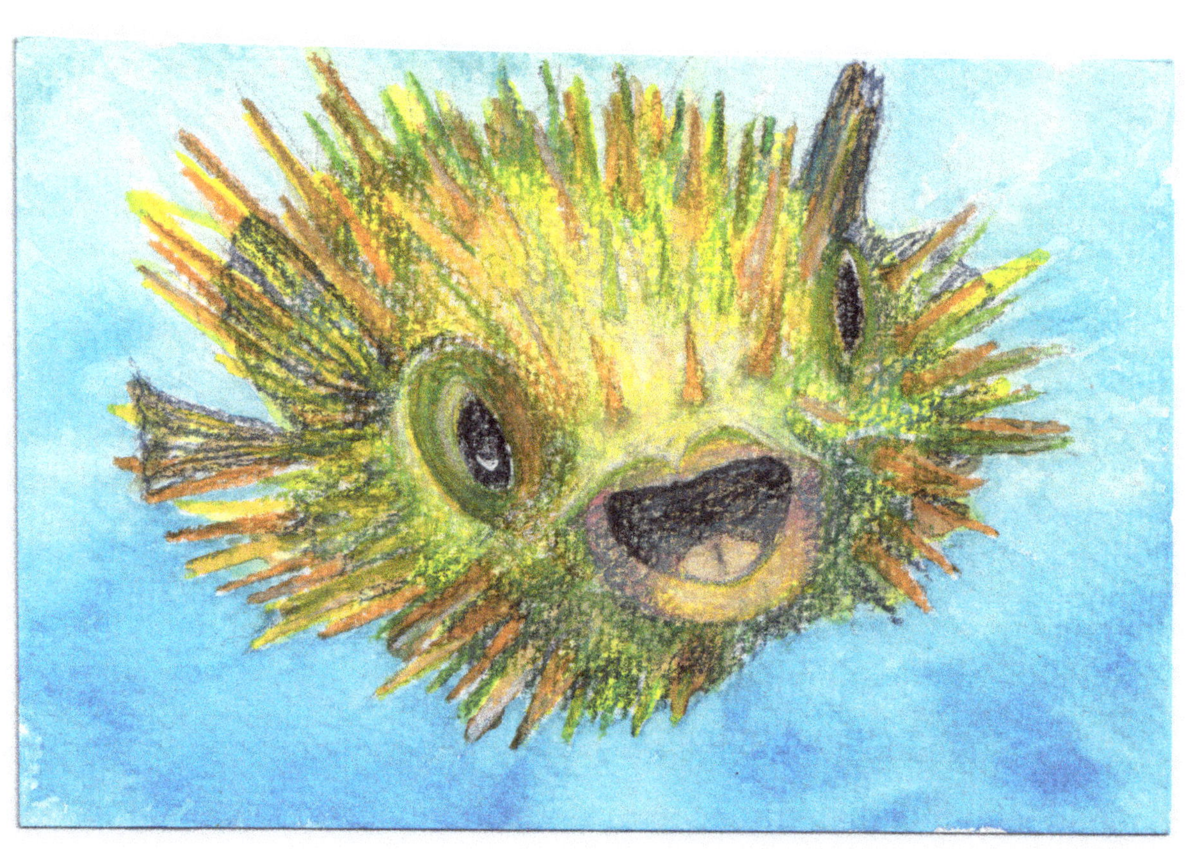

Remembering to Breathe

Breathing in 1-2-3-4 and out 1-2-3-4 calms the mind and drives down our nervous system, easing tension and moving us towards a state of relaxation. It is in this continuous and rhythmic exchange of airflow that the hypnotic, magical healing power of flow happens. Through the grounding and stabilizing force of a steady breath, we can move through even the most anxiety-provoking, fearful, and uncomfortable experiences. By counteracting the fluctuations of the mind and discombobulated forces of environmental energies, the breath helps us find ease and grace in any situation.

But what happens when we begin gasping for air, fearing that we cannot get enough? Is there enough? Are we enough? When we live in scarcity, always believing there is a shortage, we have lost trust in the abundance of the universe and ourselves. A one-sided gasping breath that only takes in air lacks the counterbalance of the released breath. And like a pufferfish, we begin to expand and fill ourselves with poisonous toxins until we have the toxic power of a pufferfish to kill thirty humans.

For the pufferfish, this expansion is intended as a form of protection. For humans, this expansion of toxins has the reverse effect of intoxicating and poisoning us. Like pent-up, unexpressed feelings towards someone else, we turn these toxic emotions on ourselves, ingesting them until we become so inflated that we explode.

If, however, in the moments of gasping for air or feeling ready to explode, we consciously choose to return to the steady breath of, in 1-2-3-4 and out 1-2-3-4, we can bring ourselves out of panic and rage mode. By realigning with the rhythmic, calming flow of the breath, we return to the present moment. It's there, deeply rooted in trust, that we are able to reconnect with the feeling of abundance and peace in ourselves and the universe.

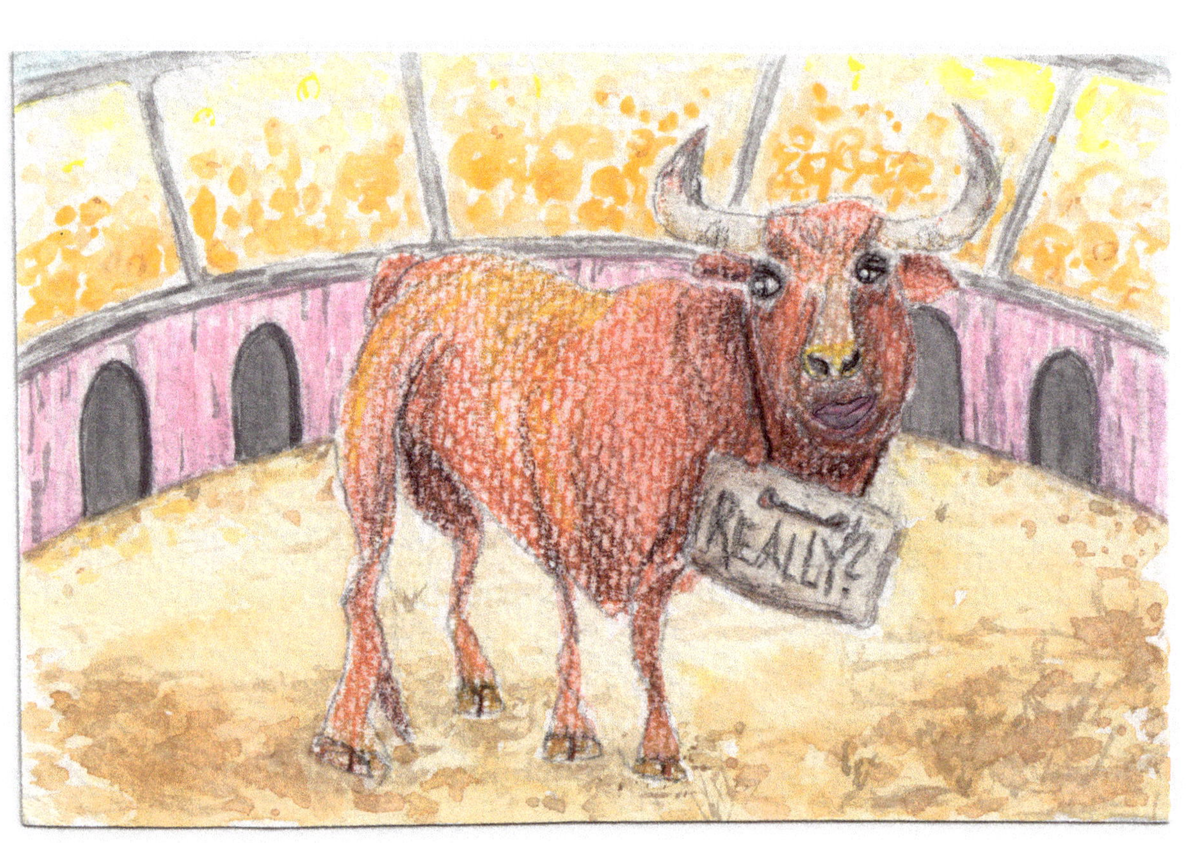
REALLY?

REALLY?

We say "REALLY?" to express a feeling of surprise or disbelief. Synonymous with "bull - shit," this feeling is all too often thought in our head. Sometimes merely hinted at through a facial expression, but rarely an authentic communication through words. Kept inside to avoid conflict or because we are unsure whether it's warranted, embodying the expression "Speech is silver. Silence is gold" only leads to an unhealthy festering of feelings.

Feelings are energy. When they are captured and contained within a confined space, they will ultimately burst out. Like a charging bull busting through the gates armed with pent-up energy and horns, we, too, seek and attack the next visible target, regardless of their guilt or innocence. A captive audience may encourage and even cheer on the show, taking sides of either toro or matador, knowing that ultimately, in the end, one of the two, or even both, will die.

In a bullfight or an argument, is it not better to give both parties a chance at survival and turn the fight into a growth opportunity through a civil exchange of thoughts and feelings? How many "REALLYs" can we carry around our neck before we break down or completely break under their inherent exorbitant weight?

The next time you feel the need to embellish yourself with a "REALLY?" sign to express surprise or disbelief, embrace that moment as an opportunity. Check-in with yourself and see if there is a chance to expand and grow. Is there an open and honest exchange that you can make happen to keep your energy moving? For it is only through an open exchange of energy flow that we have an opportunity to grow.

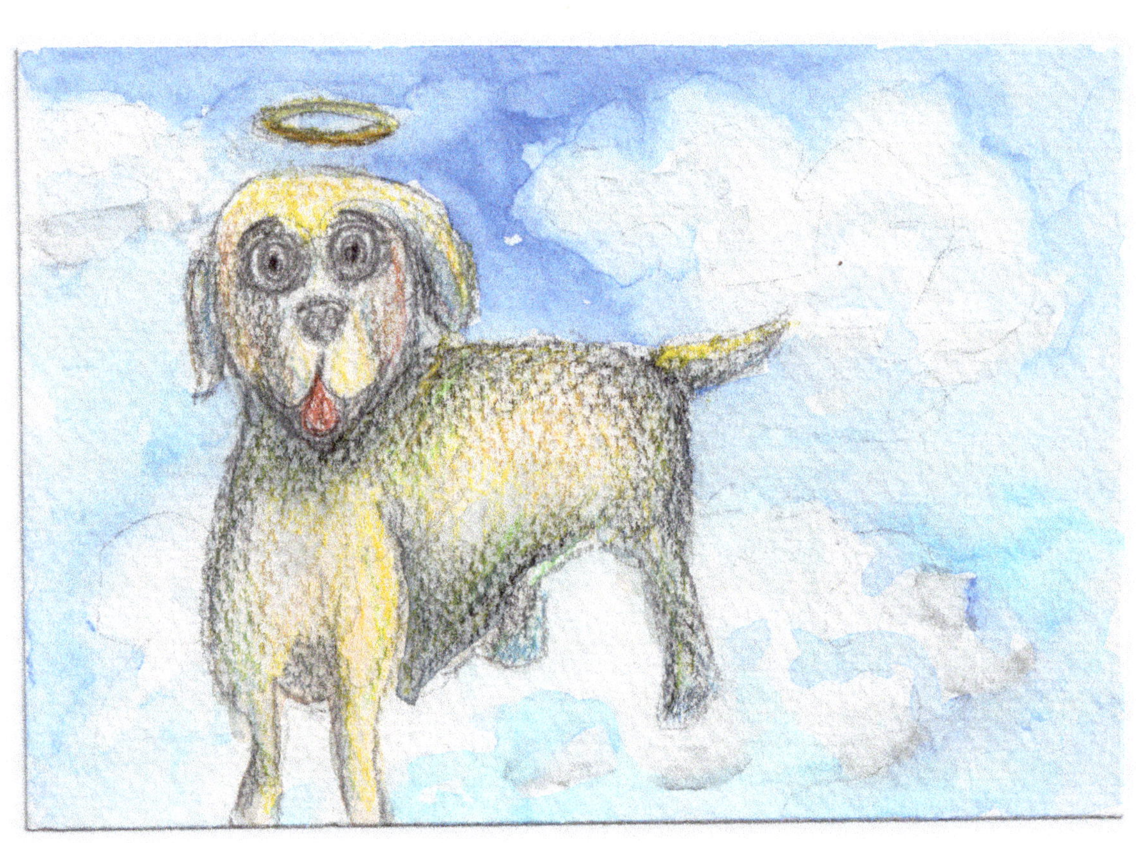

The Bones We Bury

A halo of sweetness shining brightly over the head of 'man's best friend.' One cannot deny that even the most angelic pup sometimes succumbs to her natural instinct of burying. It's her way of protecting and keeping things of value safe. Much to our dismay, the digging often occurs in places we deem inappropriate and devilishly wrong. We judge and feel the need to punish this instinctual act. Yet, the burying of bones is no different from what we humans do with aspects of ourselves and our lives that we want to keep hidden. We bury them as well for the purpose of protection, safe keeping, or out of shame.

We all have bones, our so-called skeletons in the closet, that we try to hide. Those aspects and stories of who we are that we label as devilish and whose very existence contradicts the angelic side we present to the world. However, if we allow our bones to stay buried for too long, we may forget they exist. Or we may yearningly search for them one day only to learn that we can no longer find them.

The emotional bones we bury are as much a part of who we are as the 206 bones that comprise our physical skeleton. Through the gentle, often painful process of searching, finding, and re-membering those parts of ourselves we once dis-membered and buried that we become whole again, enabling our halo to shine with angelic authenticity.

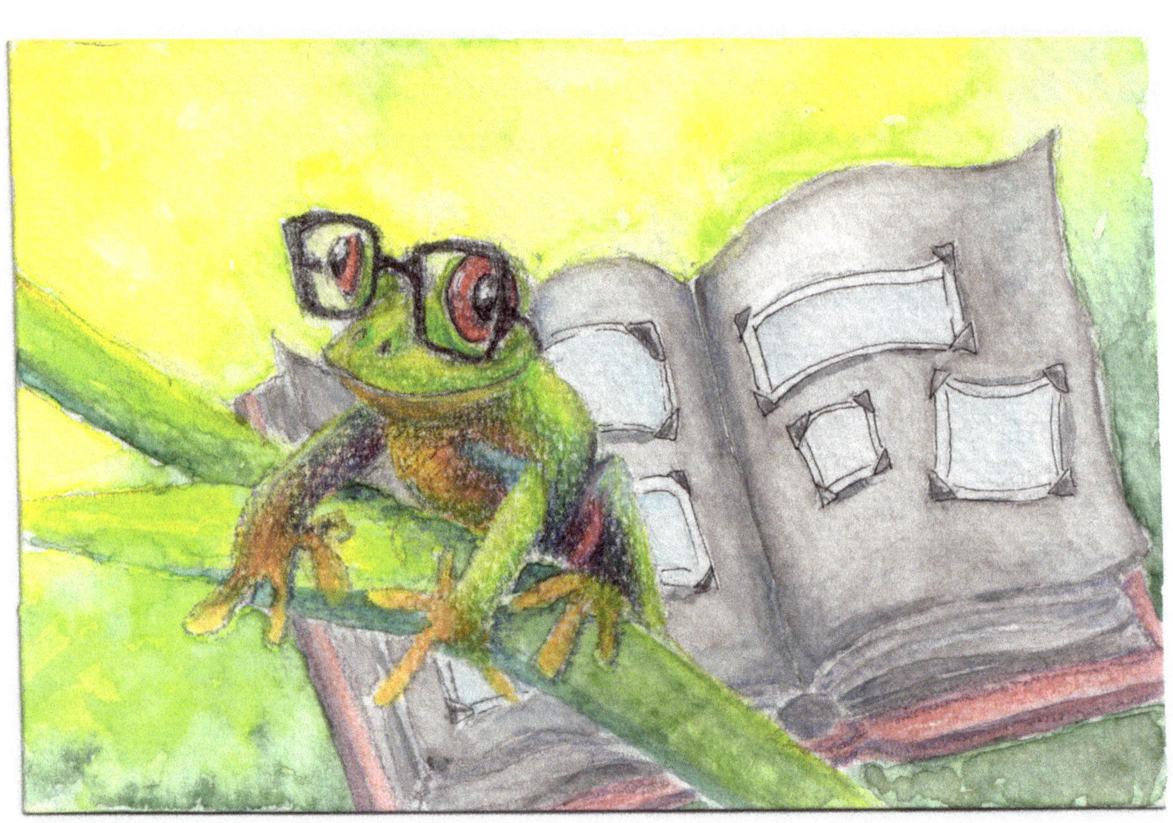

I Can Hardly Believe My Eyes

Photo albums, memory books, journals, and sketchbooks are ways for us to preserve the precious moments of our life. Their content serves as a reminder of the kind of life we are living and how we spend our time in this world. Often, hours, days, weeks, and years go by, and although we believe ourselves to be living mindfully in the moment as we record people, places, and events in our hearts and books, something happens that causes us to pause and wonder, where the time has gone.

Seeking solace in the time whirlwind of life, we pull out those sacred books for orientation and grounding. Perusing the pages, we relive, reflect, and remember the snapshot moments, those single individual elements that comprise our life. This process of re-membering, a putting together of parts, enables us to connect and make whole again the disconnected parts of our multifaceted life. When viewed through a retrospective lens, we realize that the once seemingly fragmented and random events of our lives are connected by one common and continual thread.

In the thread, we find meaning, purpose, and understanding in our lives. When we close the book, we are at peace because we have seen and can appreciate that the individual elements in our story were all part of a greater whole. Like the eyes on a frog, books give us an enhanced field of vision. They transform our 180-degree human vision into the 360-degree vision field of a frog so that we can see where we have been, where we currently are, and where we want to go.

A photo album reflection gives us the opportunity to look at how we want to be remembered in this life. We have the chance to check in and ask ourselves, is the way I am living my life aligned with how I want to be remembered? Will the snapshot moments in my sacred book tell the correct and complete story of who I am when the final chapter of my life says "The End"?

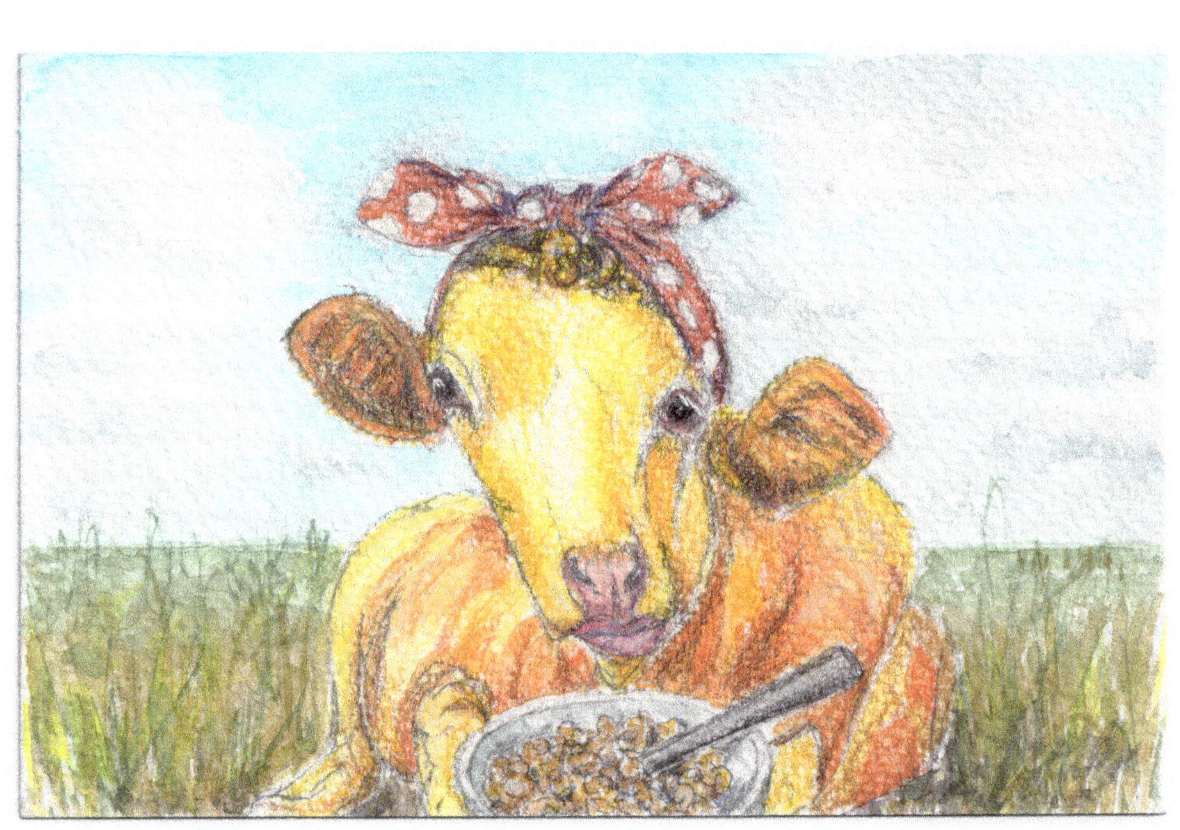

Rosie the Cereal Eating Cow

Sometimes, it's OK to have a bowl of cereal for dinner. I would go as far as to say that sometimes it's NECESSARY to give yourself permission to have a bowl of cereal for dinner.

Inspired by Rosie the Riveter, perhaps the most iconic image of American working women in the World War II era and a star of the feminist movement, Rosie the cereal-eating cow is a reminder that even in today's modern world, a second work shift of household and family responsibilities continues to be the duty of a woman. The personal and financial freedom gained by entering the workforce over half a century ago has nevertheless continued to confine us with such second-shift responsibilities as putting dinner on the table after a long day of work.

Feeling stressed, overly exhausted, and unsure what to put on the table for dinner one evening, a dear friend just beginning her day in a timezone nine hours away said, "sometimes it's OK to have a bowl of cereal for dinner." Like magic, her morning words of wisdom sprinkled my dark evening world with magical fairy dust. Although we did not have cereal for dinner that night, there have been several freeing cereal dinners since then.

Rosie, the cereal-eating cow, is a reminder to give ourselves permission to let go of perfectionism. We do not have to do and be everything for everyone all the time. Furthermore, it is not only "OK" to have cereal for dinner, but a necessity in order to give ourselves personal space and time. May Rosie and her cereal fill your bowl with the nourishing strength, courage, and empowerment you need.

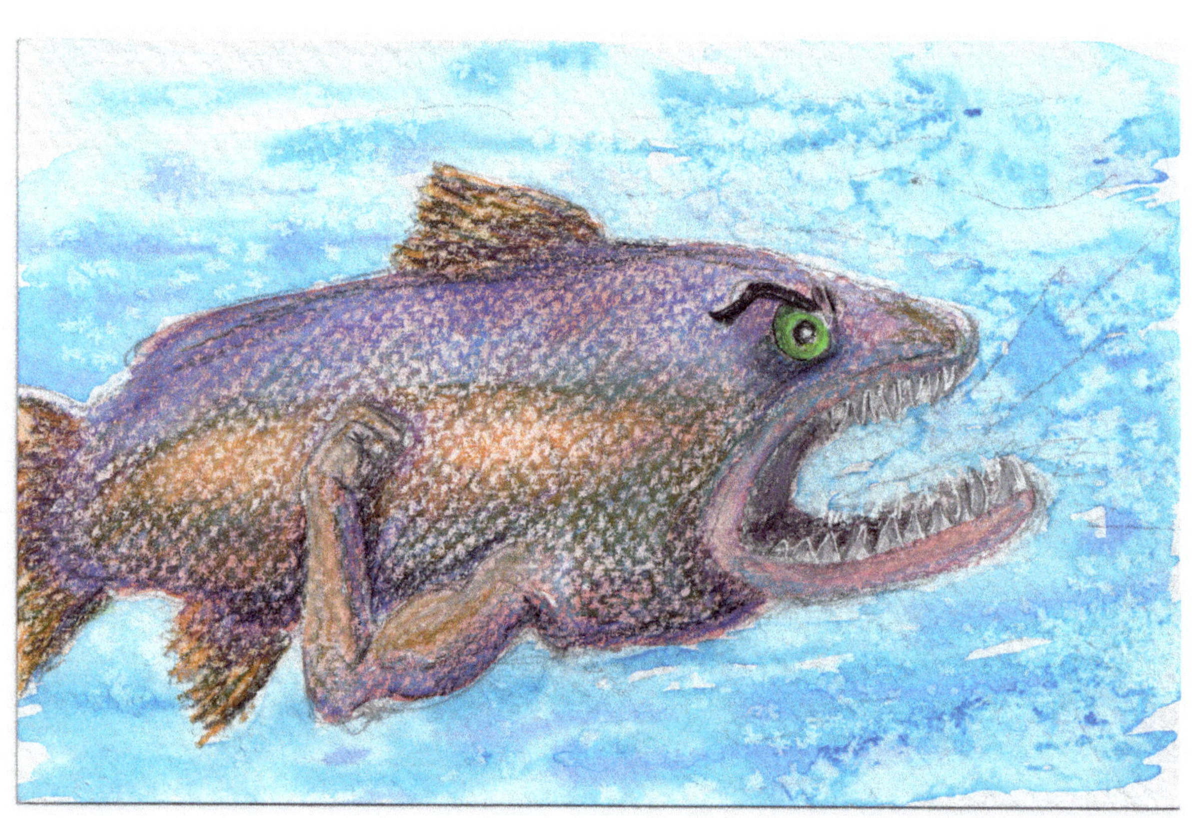

Muscling Upstream

It is widely known that salmon instinctually set forth annually on the challenging and arduous journey of swimming upstream for spawning purposes. A lesser-known fact about this migration is the influence of the earth's electromagnetic field on their journey, which enables them to travel long distances with an understanding of where they are going.

The feeling of swimming upstream is something to which we, as human beings, can relate. The force of the water current reflects societal pressures, and swimming is our journey in life. As we find our way in the world, we often find the need to flex our muscles, maybe even throw a punch or two, to get to where our ego tells us we should go. Forcefully muscling our way to the top of the class, a company, or a community. Angrily instilling our belief, will, or opinion on others. We become so focused with determination that our vision becomes short-sighted and narrow. Sometimes we find ourselves swimming in a direction completely out of alignment with where we are meant to be going. And if or when we do finally arrive at the place that was our goal, we are too exhausted to enjoy it.

Conversely, there are moments in life where we find ourselves so in the natural flow of life that the tension in our muscles releases, the expression of strain on our faces relaxes, and the clenched determination in our eyes loosens. We float with ease and grace to exactly where we are meant to be.

Neither experience should be judged as good or bad, right or wrong. Rather view each one as an opportunity to gather information, observe, reflect, and evaluate. Are your swimming techniques, the direction you are going, and the tools you are using for orientation aligned with the electromagnetic fields of your inner earth, the energetic forces of your heart and soul?

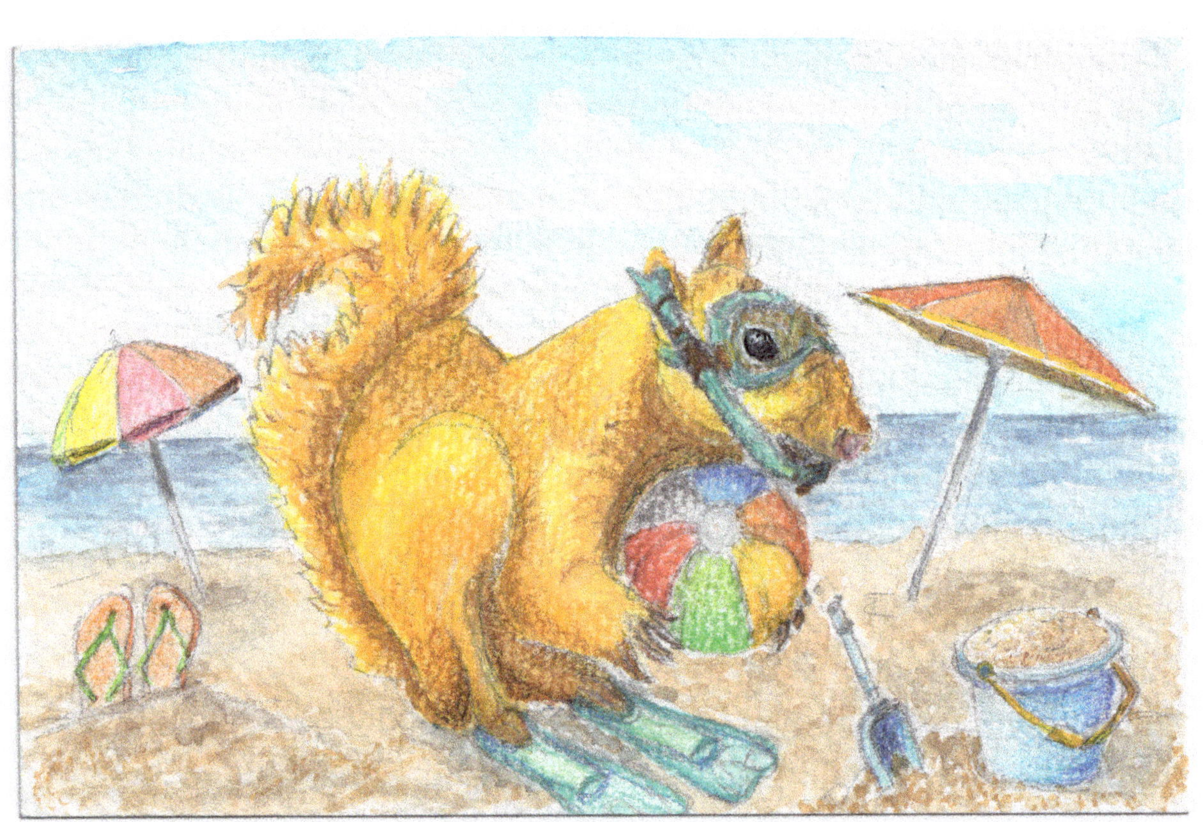

Seasons of Life

Summer, like all seasons, is a period of time. It is not separate from but rather linked to the previous and subsequent times of spring and fall, both of which embrace the season of winter. We continually move through the temporary yet predictable qualities of each season, knowing that one would not be possible without the other. For one ultimately prepares and leads to the next.

So too, are the seasons of our life. Like a squirrel who has gathered and stored his supply of nuts for the winter, we need to create a stash of nourishment to feed ourselves during the colder and darker phases of our life. Rather than the edible nuts of a squirrel, the little nuggets of nourishment that we collect are tiny acts of self-care that we can digest when darkness surrounds us. If we do not put forth the effort of finding and storing them in the fall, we risk starving ourselves in the dark of winter. Similarly, it is only by going inward into the quiet, stillness of darkness that we can move with fortitude into enlightened spring. Awakening, growing, and blossoming into full vibrant beauty in the likening image of mother nature.

Moving into summer, the transformative energies of springtime turn the nut we held in our hands two seasons ago into a colorful and playful beachball, indicative of fun! Furthermore, our nourishing winter self-care nuggets have changed into the umbrellas, flip-flops, bucket, and shovel that now adorn the landscape. With snorkel, mask, and fins, we now find ourselves equipped and eager to dive deep into the depth of the ocean as unknown waters filled with treasures are waiting to be discovered. And in this body of water, we find the chest filled with our inner bliss of who we truly are.

Seasons are a reminder of life's impermanence, and our ability to let go determines the serenity and grace with which we move through change. As summer evolves into fall, although we desperately want to hold on to that good feeling of summer fun, we learn to let go. By embracing and trusting the flow of life, like nature's four seasons, we recognize how perfectly everything is designed by a loving universe in service and support of us.

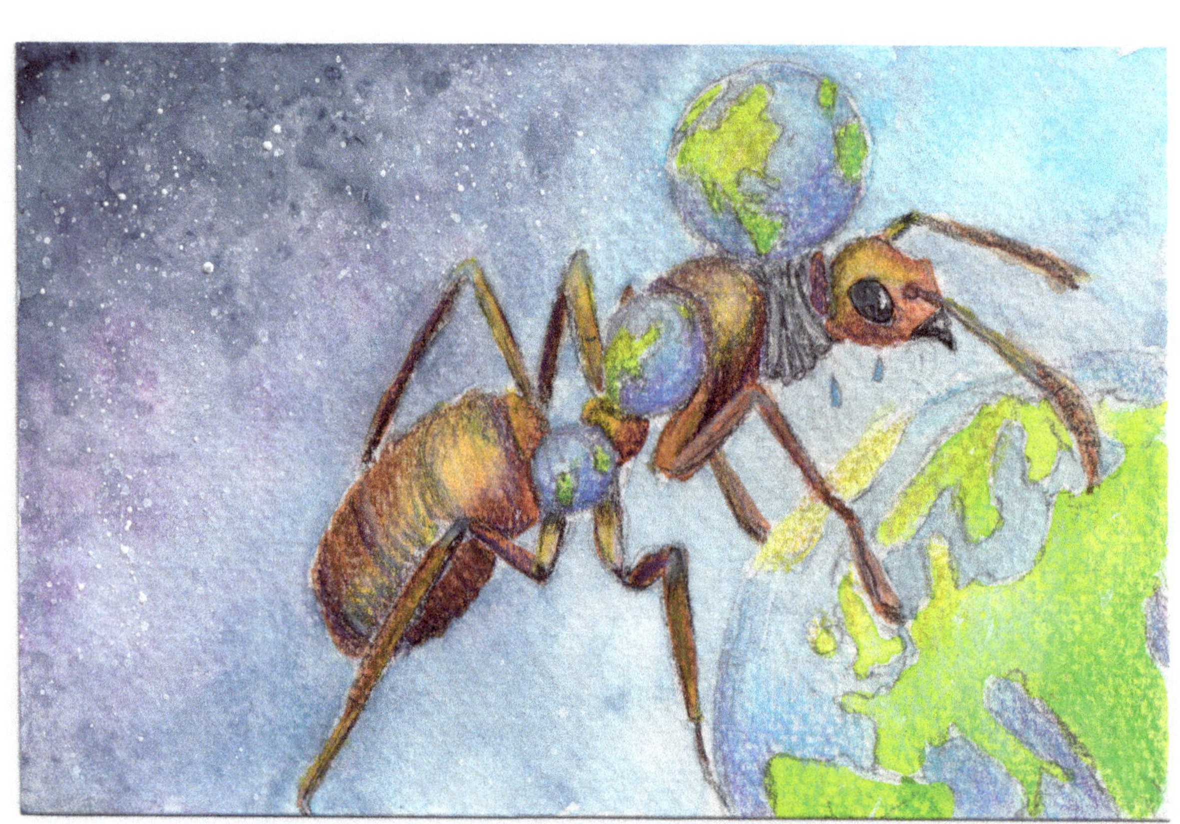

Juggler of Worlds

Strength in serenity. Small but mighty. Both are expressions of seemingly opposing concepts. An ant, small in size, is strong enough to carry between 10 and 50 times her body weight. But just because an ant is innately industrious and strong, should she be forced to carry the weight of multiple worlds?

Similarly, why do we expect ourselves to lug the additional burden of other people's worlds and allow them to develop into the joints that hold us together? Accustomed to the weight, we fear that the absence of these worlds could cause us to become disjointed and fall apart. But will we not break due to the massive weight anyway? Beginning with sweat, the first sign of exerted effort, our posture slowly changes and adapts. A bend here and a bend there accommodates and cradles the once-foreign worlds that have now become ours.

Wondering how we can manage our current load, much less muster up the strength to add even just one more, somehow, and, for some reason, we always do. Maybe it's a habit or a role we have assumed. Perhaps we have become so accustomed to the weight, even becoming stronger as a result, that we would feel uncomfortable or naked to be without. Are we attempting to fill a void or gaps we believe exist in ourselves to feel whole? Whatever the initial reason, the weight will eventually become too much. When it does, ask yourself, will the original inhabitants return to take them back, or will we find ourselves broken down and alone?

Answering these deeper questions gives us an awareness that we can filter and selectively choose the worlds we want to temporarily hold. Like juggling, where success is determined by the ability to hold and release rather than clench and grip, the key to prolonged juggling is rhythm and timing. By applying this skill set to our experience of carrying the worlds of others, we can protect ourselves from collapsing under their weight and avoid allowing them to become an enmeshed permanent part of us.

The consistent timing and steady rhythmic flow of a juggling performance remind us to receive-hold-release, receive-hold-release. 1-2-3, 1-2-3. There! Feeling lighter already?

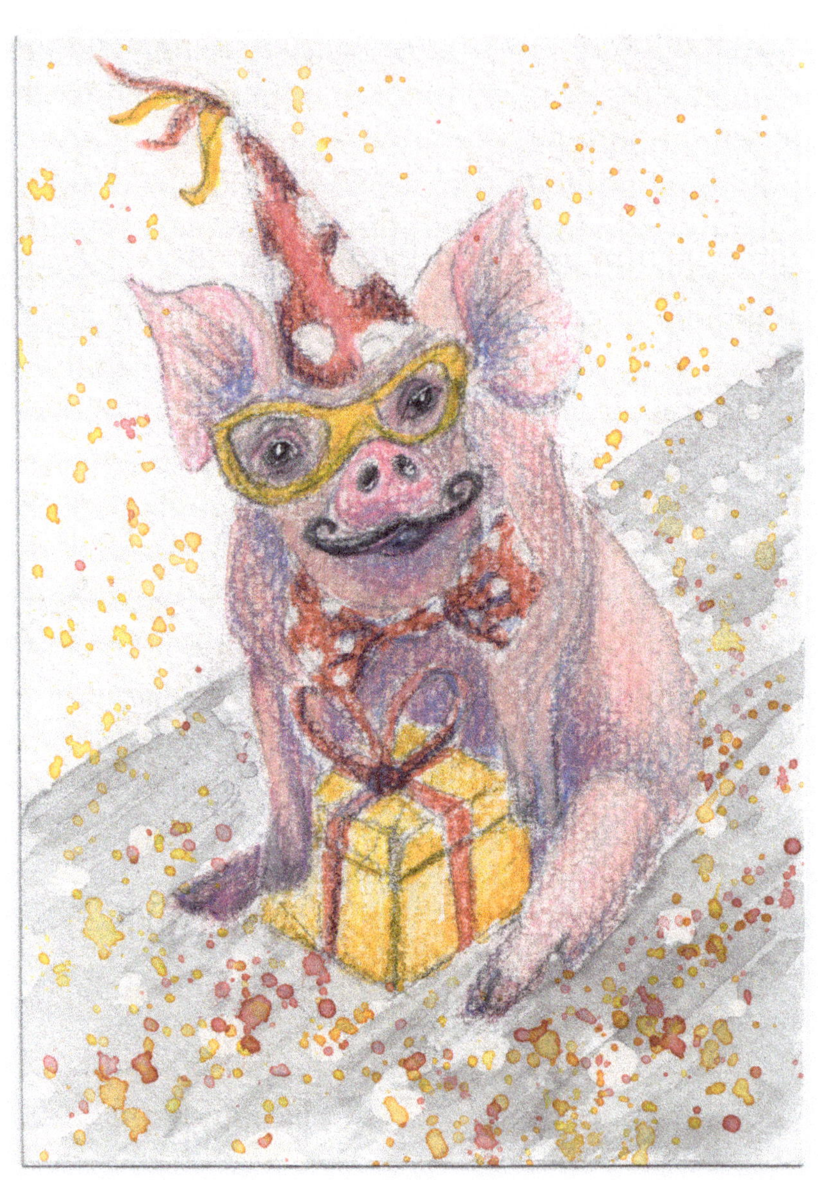

A Daily Celebration of Gratitude

Throughout time and across cultures, a pig has symbolized good luck and abundance. A gift is something that is given or received without compensation. Our greatest good fortune and most extraordinary gift is that every morning when we wake up, we receive 'the present' of a brand new day. A day to make of it what we choose. A day to celebrate being alive.

Monks begin every day on their mats by turning onto their stomachs and giving thanks to the earth. What if, before our feet touch the floor as we get out of bed, we begin our day with a moment of gratitude? An expression of appreciation for the most essential gift of the universe, for all that is and will be possible. Imagine how such a momentary brief act could change our perception of possibility and guide our vision for the 24-hour day just beginning.

When the phrase "I am grateful for…." becomes a daily mantra, it helps us to see and live in possibility. As the light from the morning sun is shining through a window, gratitude illuminates our path. Reciting a mantra offers us ease and momentum, like sliding down a hill on newly fallen pure white powder snow. Every day is a celebration. In the fortuitous spirit of a pig, we get to experience the abundant offerings of a new day. We get to choose the color, style, and amount of confetti we sprinkle into our lives. We get to choose the hat we want to wear and the person we want to be. We make the choice if what we bring to the 'party of life' in the gift box will be given with intention, aligned with who we are and why we are here, or if our gift box will be empty, waiting for others to determine its content.

The very moment of waking up, a brand new day with limitless possibilities, is the true present, a gift for which we should be thankful. By living in gratitude, we feel a sense of ease as we slide through life. And as we gain confidence in our natural momentum, we learn to enjoy and trust the present moment we hold in our hands. We realize how reciting the short albeit profound sentence "I am grateful for…" as part of our daily morning has changed our lives.

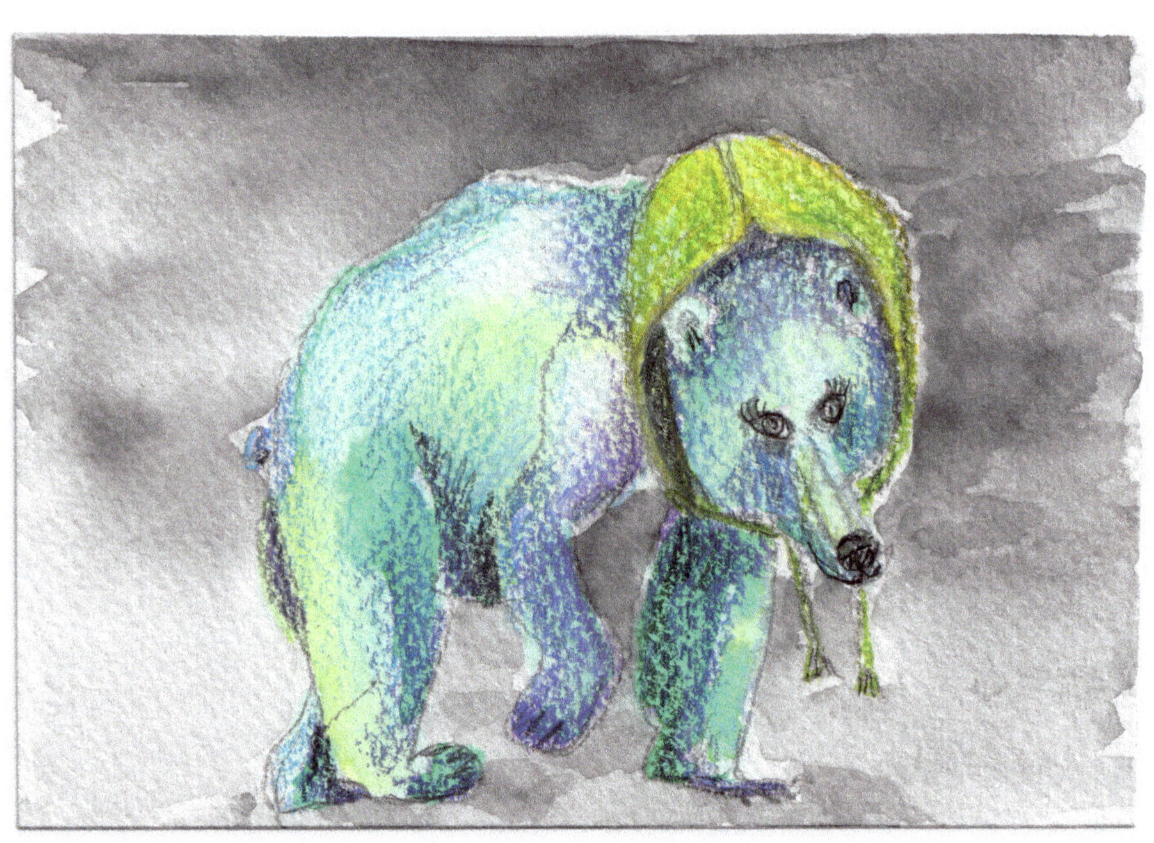

Hibernation Hoodie

As Dr. Suess tells us, some days we feel "slow and low low down." But what happens when this type of day continues over an extended period of time? When the once sporadic day of "low low down" becomes consecutive days, weeks, or even months? When this way of feeling becomes part of our routine, we find ourselves in a rut.

Although negative in connotation, a rut isn't necessarily an experience that we need to judge as such. A rut can also be of service to us by providing an opportunity to go inward and check out our current state of being. It gives us a chance to reorient ourselves and move us in the direction of our vision more mindful, reflective, and self-aware. When we feel the need to go into hibernation by pulling a hood over our heads to block out external distractions, it's our soul's way of telling us that it's time to tune out and tune in to our inner wisdom.

Routine ways of being and doing can free us up and create space for other things in our day. But they may be the exact culprit that landed us in a rut and caused us to become numb, unaware, and disconnected. Conversely, by consciously changing our routine, we can use the security of familiarity and the excitement of novelty to get ourselves out of a rut. Discover a different route to work. Taste new food. Engage in an unfamiliar activity. Befriend a stranger. By shifting even just one element in our routine, we activate the laws of physics, which state that an object will not change its motion unless a force acts on it. The movement inherent in cause-effect relationships releases us from the binding forces of being stuck in a rut.

So the next time you are feeling "low, low, down," welcome it as a chance to pause, examine, and reroute your routines. When you feel ready, remove the safety and comfort of the hibernation hood. Wake up to a revitalized and energized you, ready to embrace a new day filled with undiscovered moments of beauty and magic.

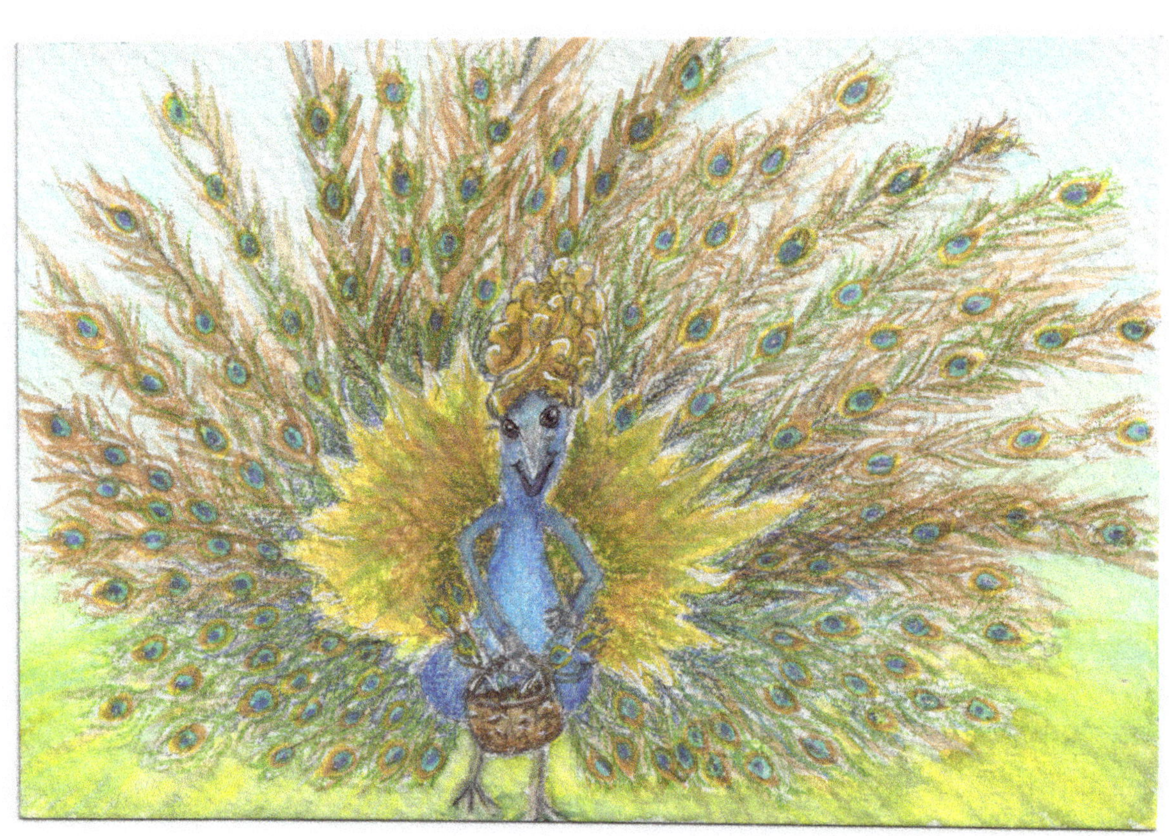

Spreading Beauty

The peacock spreads his feathers as a form of communication and to attract mates. The splendid display of feathers in iridescent hues of blue, green, yellow, and brown is a sight of pure beauty to behold. It's no wonder nature has designed the fan this way. After all, it ensures the procreation of the peacock species. Unfortunately, the beautiful feathers are also coveted by humans and, as a result, are illegally poached. Hunted for meat and the value of their breathtaking feathers, green peacocks have landed on the endangered species list.

Rather than eyeing others and envying them, we should turn our focus inward to discover our own beauty and find ways to share it. The artist Pablo Picasso once said, "The meaning of life is to find your gift. The purpose of life is to give it away." What makes you beautiful, and how are you spreading that beauty into the world? We all have gifts, something of value to share. Every day is an opportunity to give this gift through our thoughts, words, and actions.

So, fan out your beauty and share it generously. Be mindful in your offering and give from a place of abundance. But don't be wasteful. When you feel like your beauty is being poached by greedy, envious others, remember that it is okay, even necessary, to withdraw. Set boundaries and take the time to replenish. Protect and restore your resources. And remember, these self-care practices will enable you to resurface when the time feels right. Rejuvenated, you will once again be able to resume your purpose of spreading beauty.

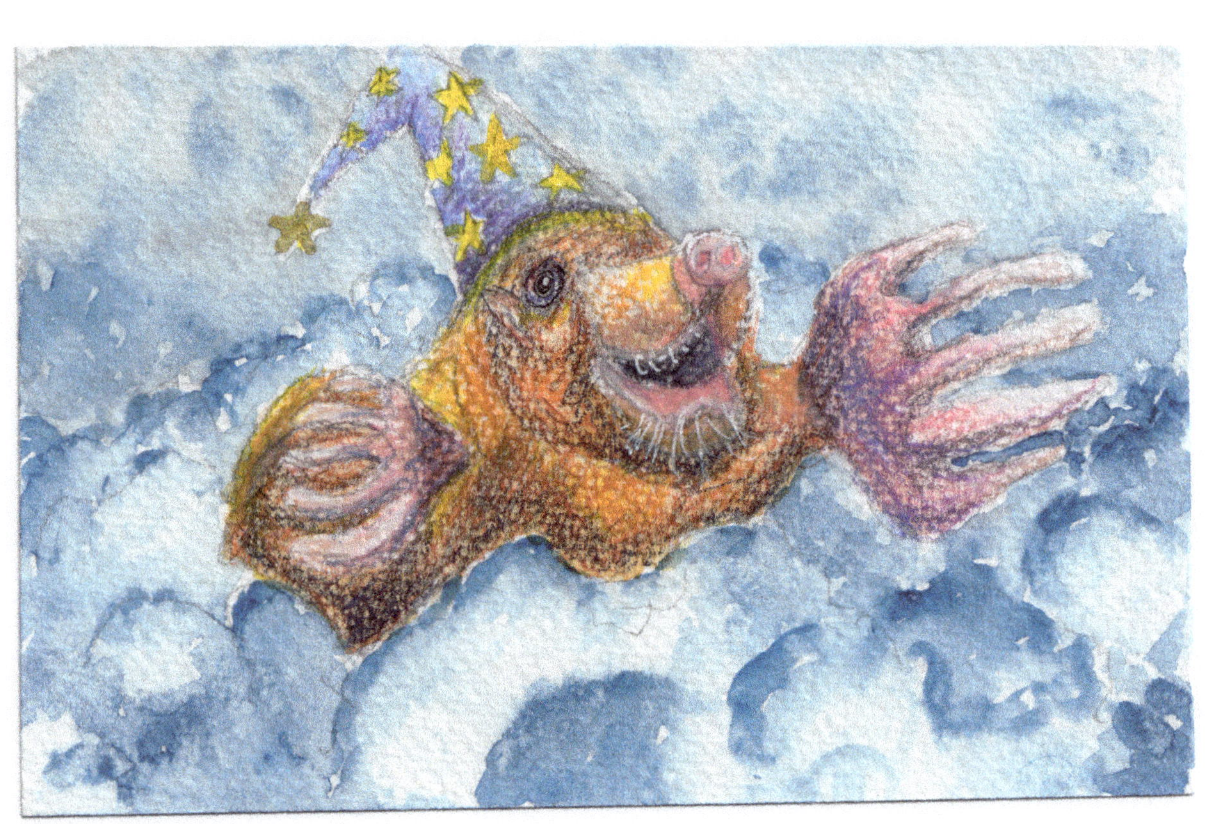

A Matter of Perspective

Garden parties are not just for human beings. Mammals, such as moles, quite enjoy a grand old party in our garden as well. While we, as gracious hosts, are busy preparing surface areas above ground with flowers, lawn chairs, and drinks, the mole is enjoying his own party beneath our feet underground.

From our perspective, the little volcanoes of dirt indicate that we are not the only ones having a party. To us, they are an eyesore in our perfectly groomed garden and pose a tripping hazard to our party guests, especially those in high heels. From the mole's perspective, he is providing us with full-service soil aeration free of charge. Not to mention the gratuitous removal of destructive insects and plant-eating slugs. All this is in return for a little fine dining of earthworms and other small invertebrates found along the way. Not a bad deal, right?

A pest from the human perspective is an altruistic savior from the mole's perspective. Frantically searching for ways to remove our happy undercover cohabitant, we try flooding the tunnels with a garden hose only to realize our efforts are merely party-crashing actions rather than a shutdown as we had intended. And so the mole continues to party unphased, and his joy of digging and dining heightens. Meanwhile, our irritation intensifies, and we begin making a "mountain out of a molehill" and exaggerate the dangers posed by our cohabitator.

A change in perspective and empathy can help us see the garden party from the viewpoint of a mole. We might even recognize that a party is a moment of joy, regardless of who is attending and where it takes place. A party's joy is to be shared in peace, not in adversarial fighting. After all, right or wrong, friend or foe, over or under the surface, are all a matter of perspective.

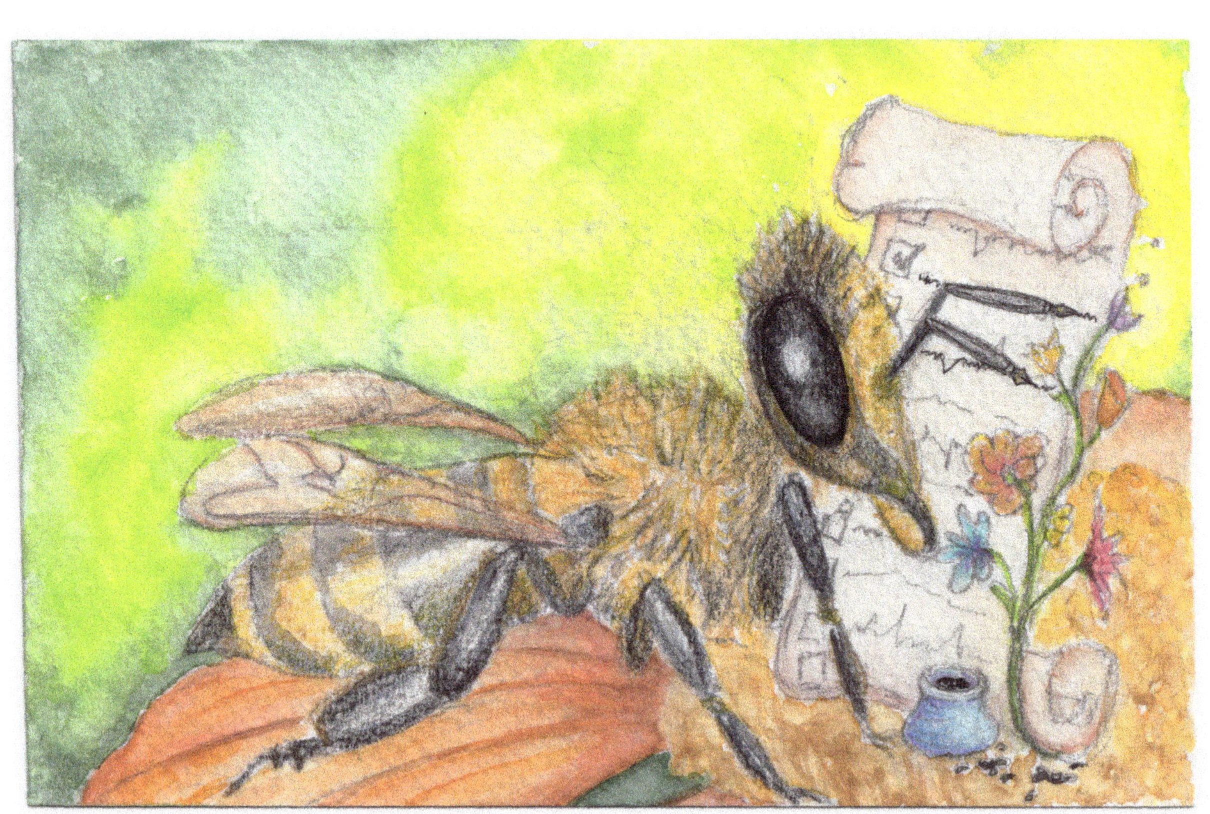

Finding Bee-auty in Bee-ing

Constantly busy, filling our lives with an insatiable need to do, accomplish, and complete. Why do we find such satisfaction in doing rather than being? Why is it that we choose to give our feelings of self-worth over to the often fleeting and brief moments when we experience task completion satisfaction? Should the pleasure of that glorious and triumphant, albeit short-lived, experience of a job really command how we feel about ourselves?

When we describe our day as busy, although a lot is happening, it often ends up feeling draining and, in the end, empty. When we choose to describe a busy day as full, we have the power to shift from draining to nourishing. Like feeling physically full after eating a meal, a full day can leave us feeling soul nourished.

So, what would happen if we bravely detached ourselves from our addiction to doing and shifted our focus to bee-ing? Is it not our well-bee-ing that gives us a feeling of worthiness rather than the things we are tasked with doing?

Celebrate the beauty of being and bee-ing YOU. Stop glorifying the things you do. They may keep you buzzing and busy, but they also keep you spinning and small. Doing is only a mirage that is defying the being of who you are! Give yourself permission to be the queen bee rather than the worker bee because, unlike the industrious worker bee who only receives royal jelly during the first two days of her existence, the queen bee, simply by bee-ing, receives the nourishment of royal jelly an entire lifetime!

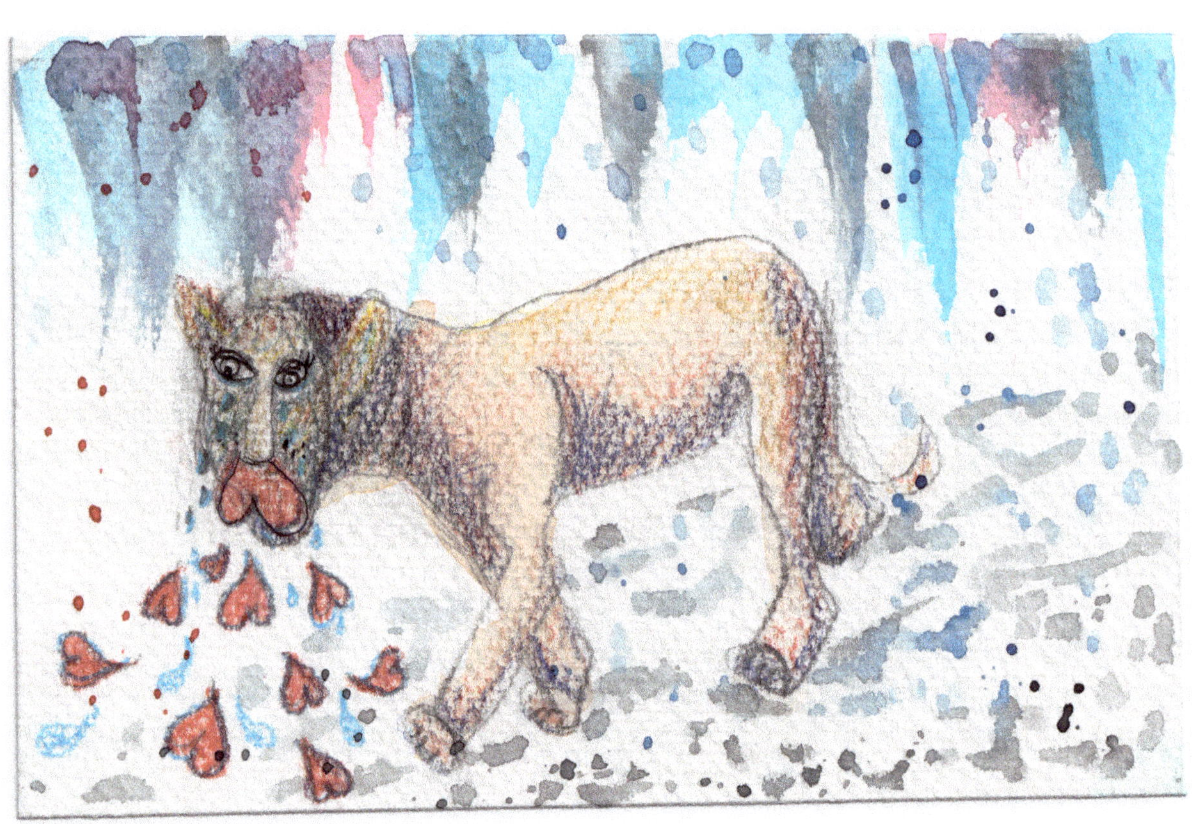

The Dark Side

We all have a dark side, a part of us we want to keep secret and hidden from the world and ourselves. That part of us we so desperately want to dissociate from or even deny its existence. We habitually refuse to acknowledge and feel, much less share it with the world. The shamed relationship to this part of ourselves is the result of conditioning we have experienced.

Throughout our lives, we have learned to be wary of all that is unpleasant and deemed as negative. Childhood fairytales warned us about evil step-parents, poisonous potions, and telling lies. In the movie Star Wars, Yoda is quoted as saying, "But beware of the dark side. Anger, fear, aggression….easily they flow…". The confident and proud zodiac sign Leo, represented by a lion or lioness, is described as having a dark side of arrogance, vanity, and self-absorption.

But what is this dark side really, if not a part of who we are? Regardless of what we label it - unpleasant, evil, or even harmful - our dark side is as much a part of us as our bright and cheery side. It is only through the feeling, expressing, and ultimate releasing of our dark side thoughts and emotions that we find the peace of authentic wholeness.

Physically, our bodies are designed to remove irritants through nose mucus and eye tears. Although both of these natural bodily releases have also been given a negative connotation, they are essential functions of the body's cleansing system. Often frowned upon by society, these bodily releases allow us to experience the benefits of letting go. If we do not give ourselves permission to let go and continually hold onto things, we become convoluted with negativity which ultimately leads to suffering.

So the next time unpleasant feelings begin to surface, and you find yourself pushing them back down or negating them, don't shun them. Face them and give them a chance to be heard, seen, and felt in a safe space. Releasing our physical and emotional 'irritants' provides an opportunity to shift from darkness to light, fragmentation to wholeness, and illness to health.

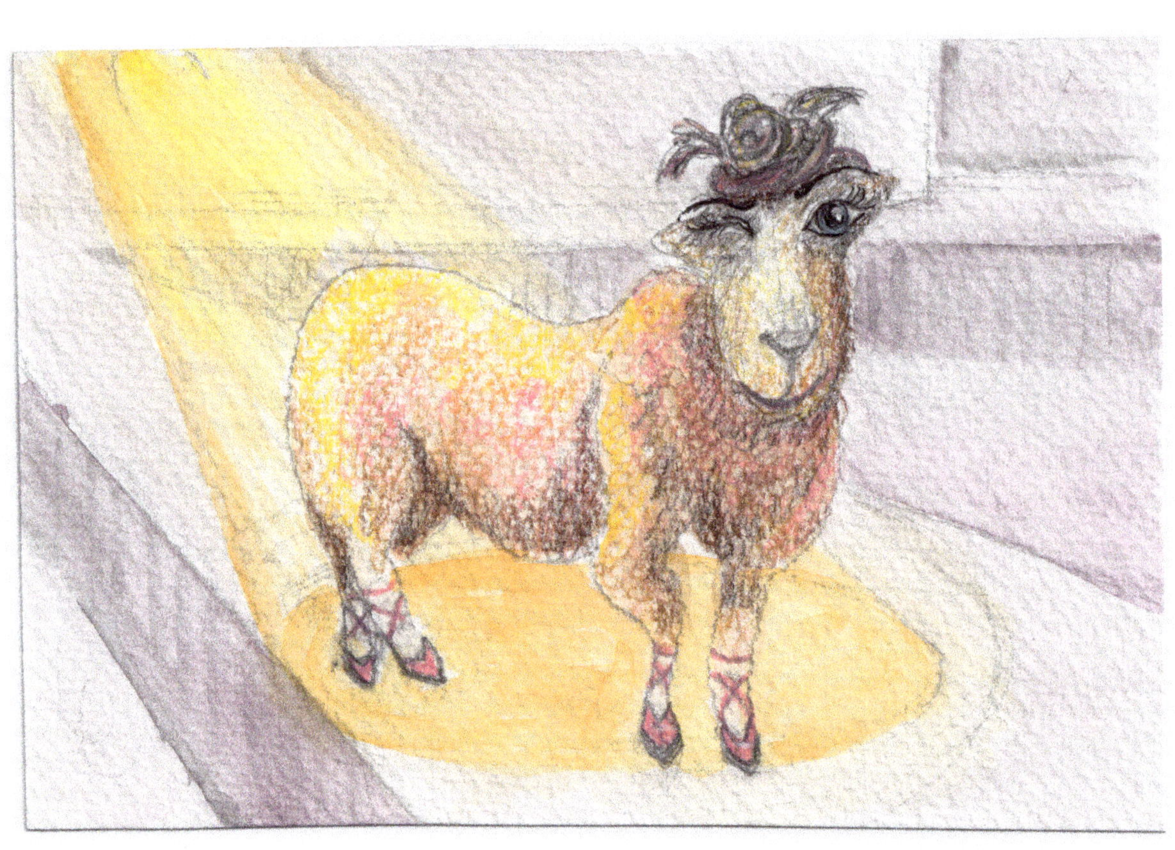

The Spotlight

"In the future, everybody will be world-famous for 15 minutes." The words of Andy Warhol remind us that a moment, perhaps our moment, in the spotlight is fleeting and brief. Fifteen minutes is, after all, only 0.00004% of an average 78-year lifespan. Of much more importance are the often invisible other 40 million minutes, or 99.99996% of our lives, that we spend out of the spotlight.

Like models on the fashion runway, their lifestyle behind the scenes, who they are out of the spotlight, defines them. Not the 15 minutes in which they stand and pose before the cameras. All that is invisible to the audience has brought them to this present moment and will accompany them long after the lights have been turned off and the show has ended.

So, don't be sheepish and embarrassed. Ask yourself, what is it that you want to be famous for? How do you want to be seen in your moment of fame on the showcased runway of life? Reflect if the life you are living, the remaining 99.99996% of your existence, is congruent with how you want to present yourself in the spotlight. Does what you show and how you spend the other 40 million minutes of your life align with your true Self and what you came into this world to share?

When it's your turn to be in the spotlight, and the light of fame shines upon you, highlighting all YOU are, revel in it. Stand tall and proud. Radiate and shine. Enjoy it! But always remember who you are. Where you came from and where you are going. Because when your 15 minutes are up, and the lights go down, you are and will always be YOU. The star of YOUR life! So go and shine your light in this world for ALL to see ALL the time!

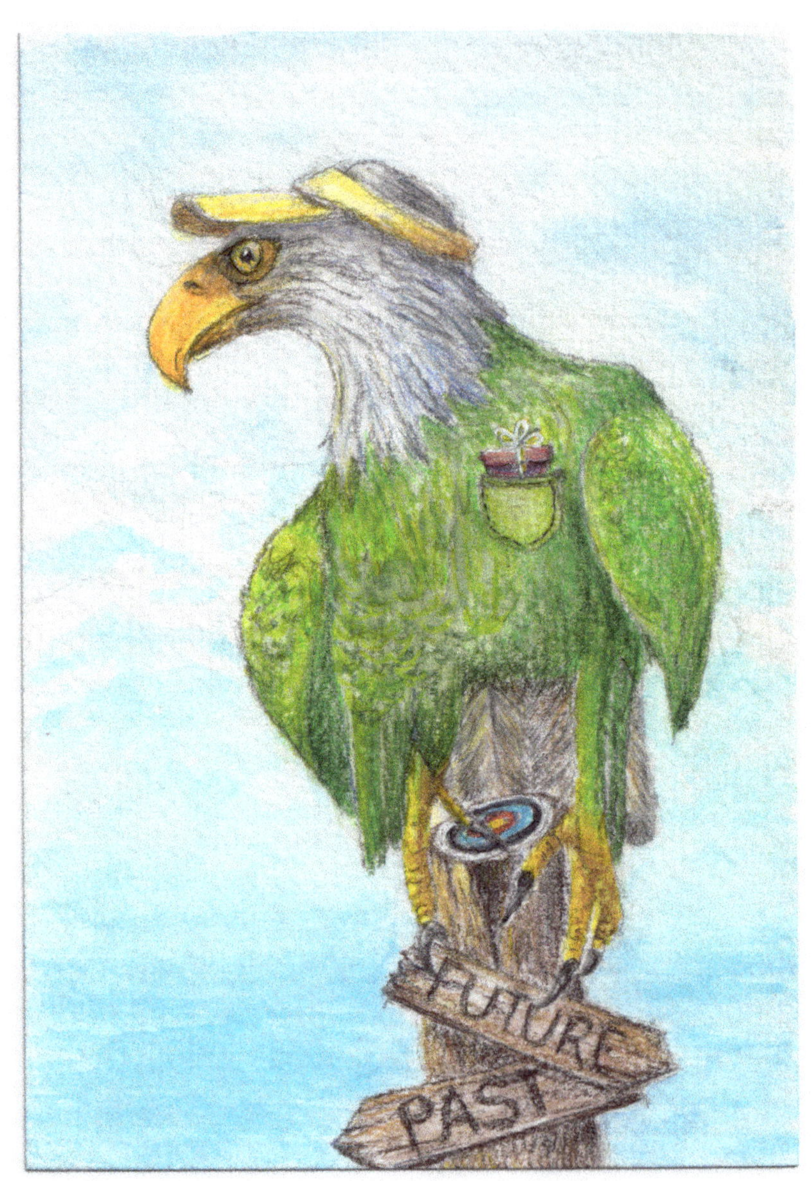

FUTURE
PAST

Bullseye

It is said that the eyesight of an eagle is 4 to 8 times stronger than that of an average human. Compared with a perfect 20/20 vision for humans, an eagle's perfect vision is 20/5. And while we see 180 degrees, eagles have an almost panoramic vision of 340 degrees.

Like an eagle, we have an innate ability to see and use our vision. But often, we cast our sight into the future with statements such as, when I…then I will … or into the past with statements like if only I had…

The trouble with focusing our gaze in either of these directions is that our hearts become filled with wishes and regrets, disguising our feelings of fear and guilt. However, when we mindfully choose to shift our focus away from future hopes and worry or past regrets and guilt, we discover that we are standing in the present, the very target our heart has been trying to lead us to.

Supported, balanced, and steady in the here and now, we perch effortlessly with peace, grace, and strength. We become aware this is where we need to be because being present IS the present. Having spent so much time and energy looking elsewhere, we have lost sight of the present in our heart-pocket waiting to be opened. Inside this box is a reminder that the bullseye of our focus, the here and now, is right beneath our feet.

From this place of center, we realize all we have been searching for outside ourselves is within us, waiting to reveal itself. Perched in centeredness, we take flight into the limitlessness of our being and find freedom in the infinite possibilities of who we are.

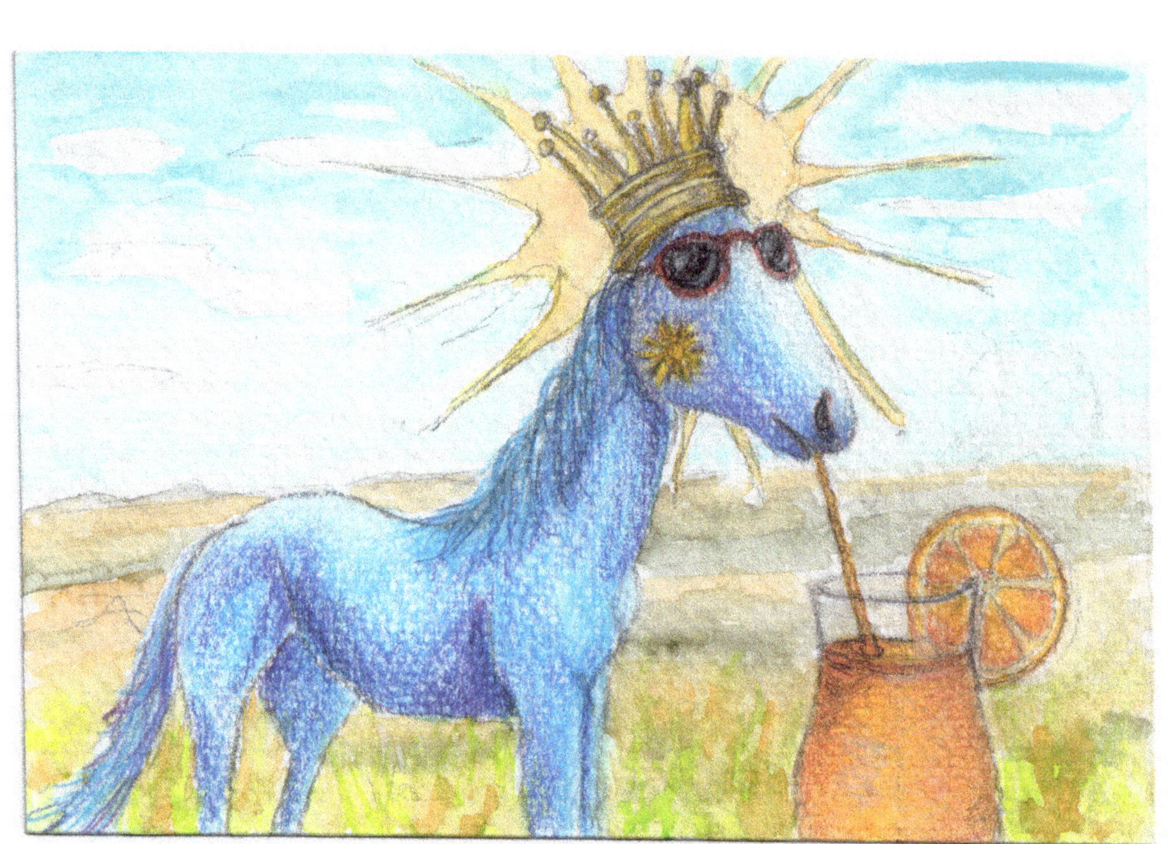

Lessons of a Pandemic

Events like the COVID-19 pandemic make history because they dramatically alter the course of what the people in the world believe to know as true. The inherent truth of how we live and what we think, feel and do. Ironically, in our search for truth, we are confronted with the reality of how many "untruths" exist and are fabricated daily at exponential rates.

In our ultimate quest for personal truth, we find ourselves confused by what to believe and what not to believe. The more we read, see, hear, and absorb through our senses, the more our search becomes convoluted. The distractions, deemed fake news by one and ultimate truth by another, come to us so rapidly and are manipulated that they are often indecipherable. The sheer task of keeping track and up-to-date with the latest information prevents us from having the time to ingest and digest all that is being piled onto our plates in overabundance.

Straight from the horse's mouth of leading authorities, we hear that Ivermectin used to deworm horses, Vitamin C found in oranges, and Vitamin D provided by the sun, can all prevent a COVID-19 infection. Whether this information is easily discernible as fake or not is not the issue. The concern is that we have a responsibility to ourselves and others to turn inward and decipher the seeds from the weeds so that we can make a conscious, informed choice as to what we allow to take root in the fields of our hearts, minds, and souls.

By sifting through the plethora of daily disseminated information, our quest for the truth will ultimately lead us to clarity, our place of peace that we are so deeply yearning for in this ever-changing and fluctuating world.

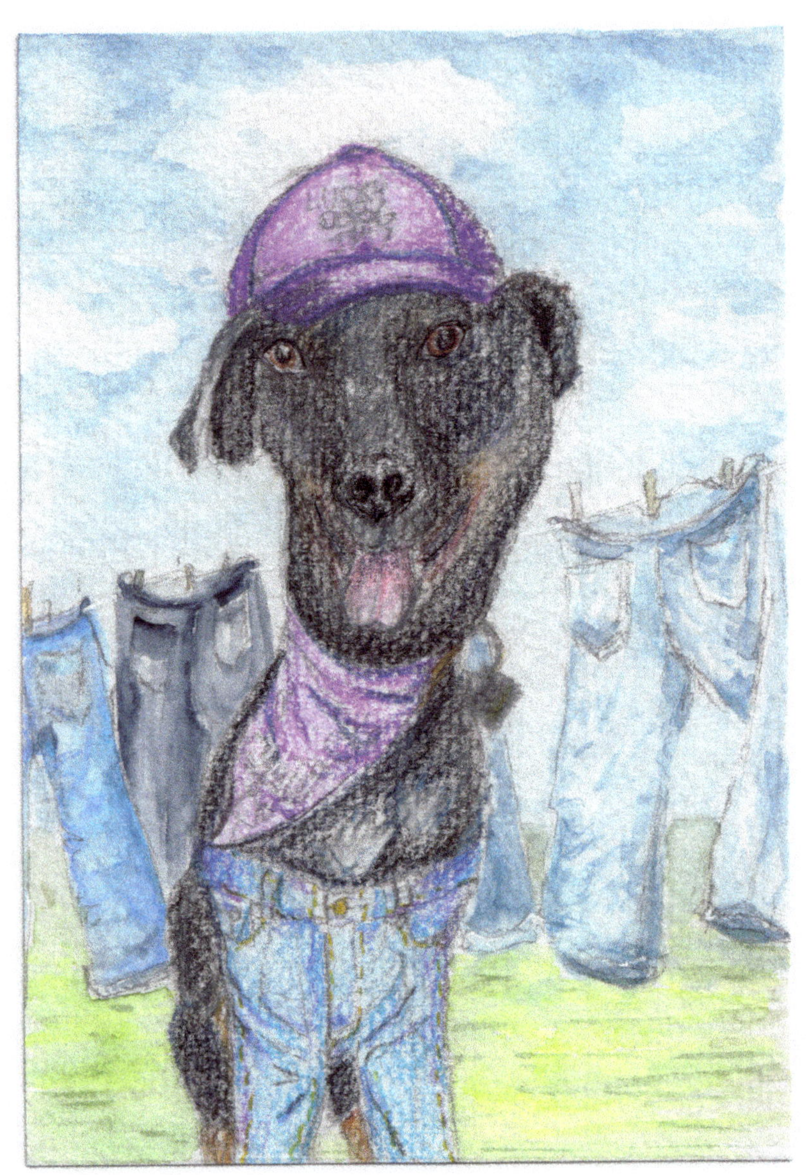

Mama Jeans

So much in life is analogous to finding the right pair of jeans. That perfect pair that simply fits and feels good. Jeans, like challenges in life, should neither be too big and difficult nor too small and easy. Sometimes we need a little extra stretch for leeway, while other times, we crave the structure of firmness. A variety of lengths support the diverse strides we take in life, while jean styles determine how much of our intimate selves we reveal. Our choice of closure regulates the ease and speed with which we let others in, and the jean color expresses our mood.

Like a circling dog nesting to arrive in the perfect position of comfort, finding the right pair of jeans is a process. It requires perseverance as we have to physically try them on in order to experience how they look and feel. Furthermore, inevitably over time, our size and fit will change. Embracing change with a sense of adventure helps us transition from the discomfort of ill-fitting, albeit familiar, jeans to the excitement of trying something new.

A willingness to let go of what no longer fits or serves us. An openness to take the risk of trying something new, not knowing if it will be a success or failure. These are two qualities of a growth mindset that will support us in not only finding the ideal jeans, but living a perfect fitting and feeling, no regrets life as well.

So the next time you find yourself in the dressing room trying on a pair of jeans, take a moment and picture this dressing room as your life. Notice, without judgment, the existing parallels between your shopping and life experiences. What can you learn about yourself? What new discoveries and information can you find? Then smile, and with self-love and gratitude, gently place them into the pocket of your new perfect-fitting jeans for safe keeping.

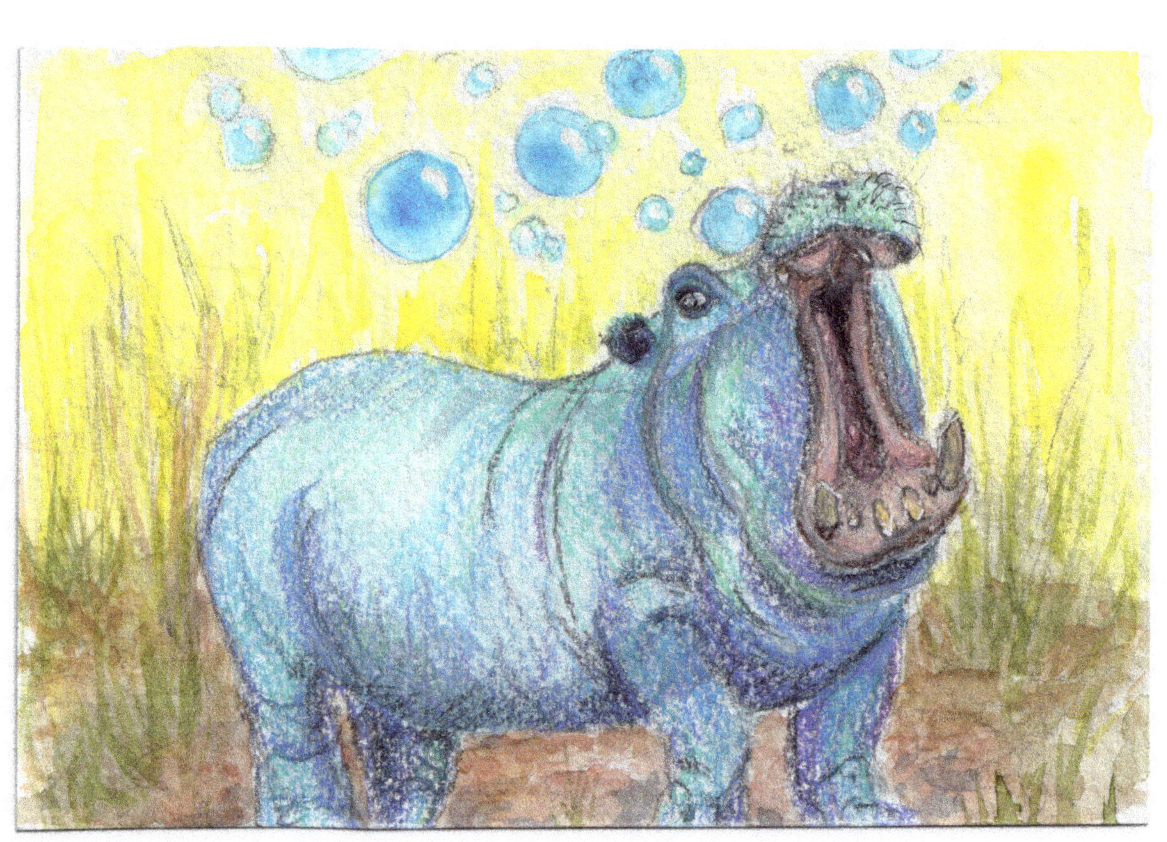

Thought Bubbles

As soap bubbles float freely through the air, light reflects on their iridescent surface, giving them a ravishing shine. Observers, mesmerized by their beauty and grace, are captivated by their fleeting existence. After only a few seconds, a little 'pop' will cause the bubbles to vanish forever! Why can't this be so with the bubbles of thoughts floating around in our heads?

When soap bubbles are blown for entertainment, we witness them from a safe, emotionally detached distance. We are free to acknowledge their presence but can also let them go just as easily, allowing us to stay grounded in the experience. But what about those bubbles in our heads that are laden with thoughts and worries? Why does the process of observing and releasing prove to be so much more challenging? Perhaps it's because the bubbles containing the thoughts are confined to our minds. Furthermore, being in such close proximity to our minds, we are unable to detach and observe our thoughts from a healthy distance. Our thoughts then become an indecipherable cluster of bubbles circulating in our minds, causing our heads to feel like they are going to explode.

Compared with the unrestricted soap bubbles slowly drifting through the air, the thought bubbles in our mind, lacking space to move freely, begin spinning in circles with frustration and anxiety. Feeling trapped, the bubbles release this energy, causing us to feel confined.

When a hippo feels threatened, they open their mouth as a warning sign to others. Similarly, a yawn is our body's way of alerting us that our brain needs renewed oxygen. On a physical level, this automatic reflex causes an air exchange that cools our brains. On a cognitive level, it brings movement to our old and stagnant patterns of thinking, creating a healthy synergy between the restless bubbles of thoughts and the mind that contains them. On an emotional level, a yawn is a way to release all that no longer serves us.

By yawning and taking the time to consciously engage with the thoughts contained in each bubble, we have the opportunity to intentionally choose either to release, pop, or examine the magical message it carries.

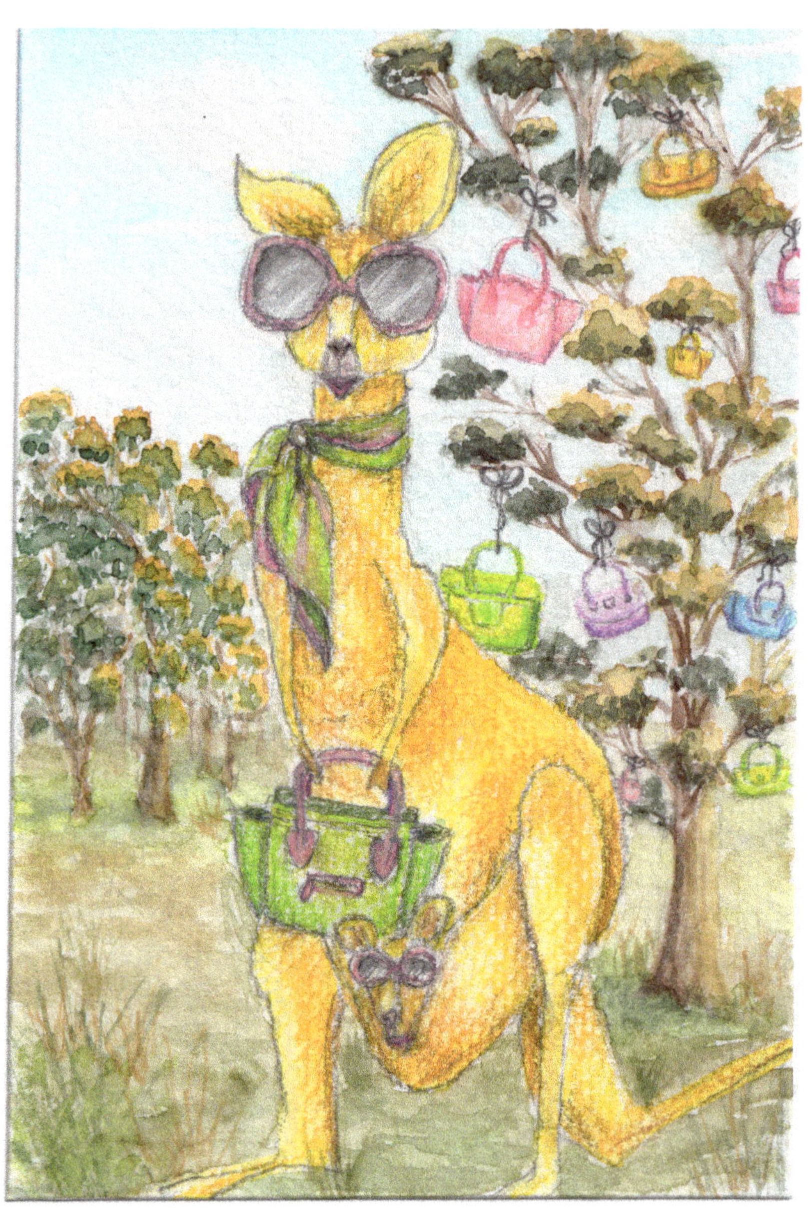

A Woman's Purse

A purse, the modern-day descendent of the woman's undergarment pocket and counterpart to the man's pants pocket is a keeper of more than material objects. In addition to the stereotypical and often erroneous red lipstick, the purse contains belongings from the owner and her loved ones. Items such as money, reading glasses, and keys, signifying material and immaterial possessions, are kept safe inside. And let's not forget that tissue for a runny nose or that cough drop to soothe a sore throat which are nestled inside for safe keeping.

The seemingly bottomless purse, a phenomenon we have all experienced in moments of panicked key searching, symbolizes a woman's boundless ability to provide and care for loved ones at a moment's notice. Unlike the restricted capacity of a physical purse, however, the emotional offering of safety and nurturance is unconditional. It far exceeds the limitations of any material object contained in the purse.

A purse, like the pouch of a kangaroo, is more than simply a pocket both in aesthetic form and apparent function. It is the personification of womanhood - strong, nurturing, always prepared to give, and yes, bottomless in these qualities. So, the next time you are in the presence of a woman's purse, approach it with love and gratitude, for what lies inside is far greater, far deeper, and far richer than anything visible from the outside.

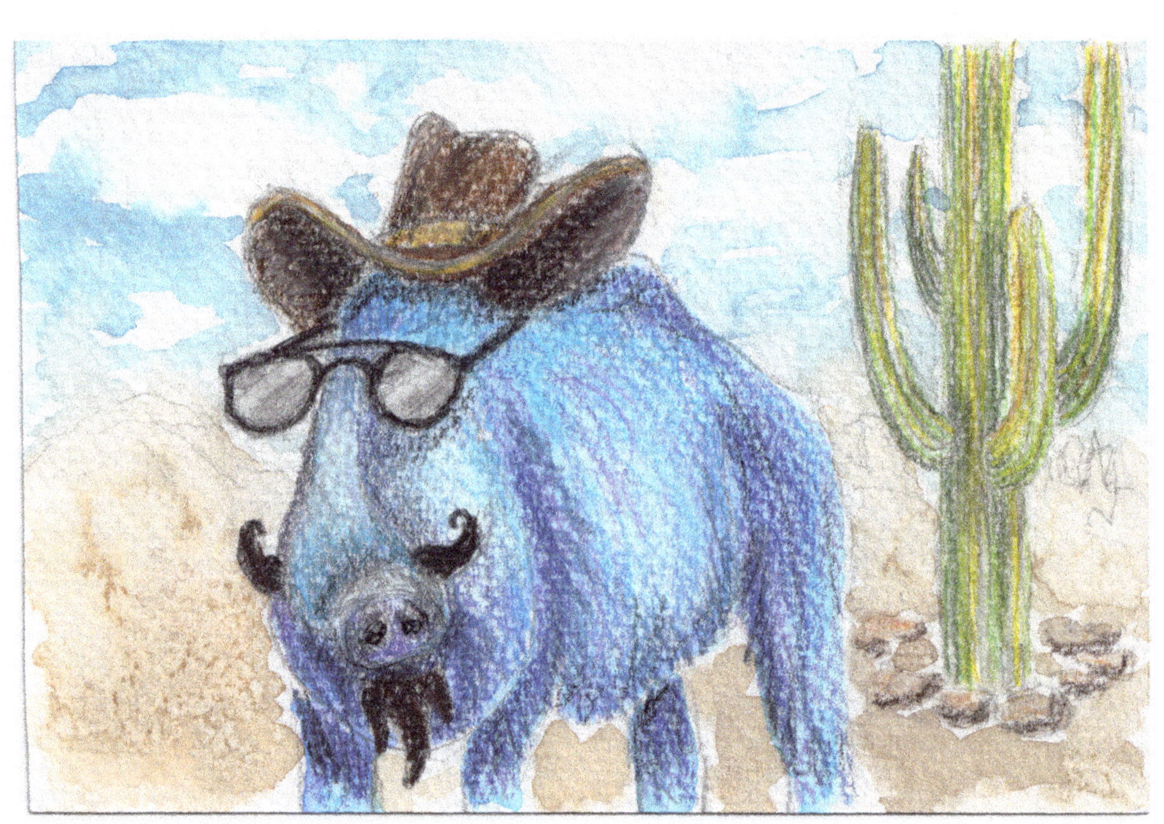

Cool as a Cowboy

There are moments in life when everything feels aligned, in harmony, and righteous. In these instances, we find ourselves embodying and emanating the feeling of being in command and control, like a boar. Standing confident and strong, we soak up and grip these feelings, wishing they could last forever. Like a cowboy who has successfully herded the cattle, sometimes with force and other times with gentle ease, we too take a breath, perhaps even with a sigh, wondering how long our herded cattle, like this perfect moment, will last.

The key, however, is not to wonder how long it will last but to thoroughly enjoy the moment. Deeply rooted in this feeling of coolness, you trust that when necessary, you will be ready and equipped to do what needs to be done because this moment has filled your bucket. Even if we try to influence and extend the duration of this feeling by wearing a wide-brimmed hat and sunglasses, the heat of the desert sun, just like the pressures of life, will eventually return, causing us to drip with sweat.

Moving between coolness and heat, it is important to remember that life is a continual interplay of ups and downs. Moments of cowboy coolness and desert sun heat follow a natural interplay. By releasing judgment and attachment to seemingly opposites of coolness and heat, like and dislike, we free ourselves to experience what is. When we stop exerting our energy for the futile task of hanging on to something that by its very nature is meant to move, we free ourselves to enjoy the ride of an undulating flow called LIFE!

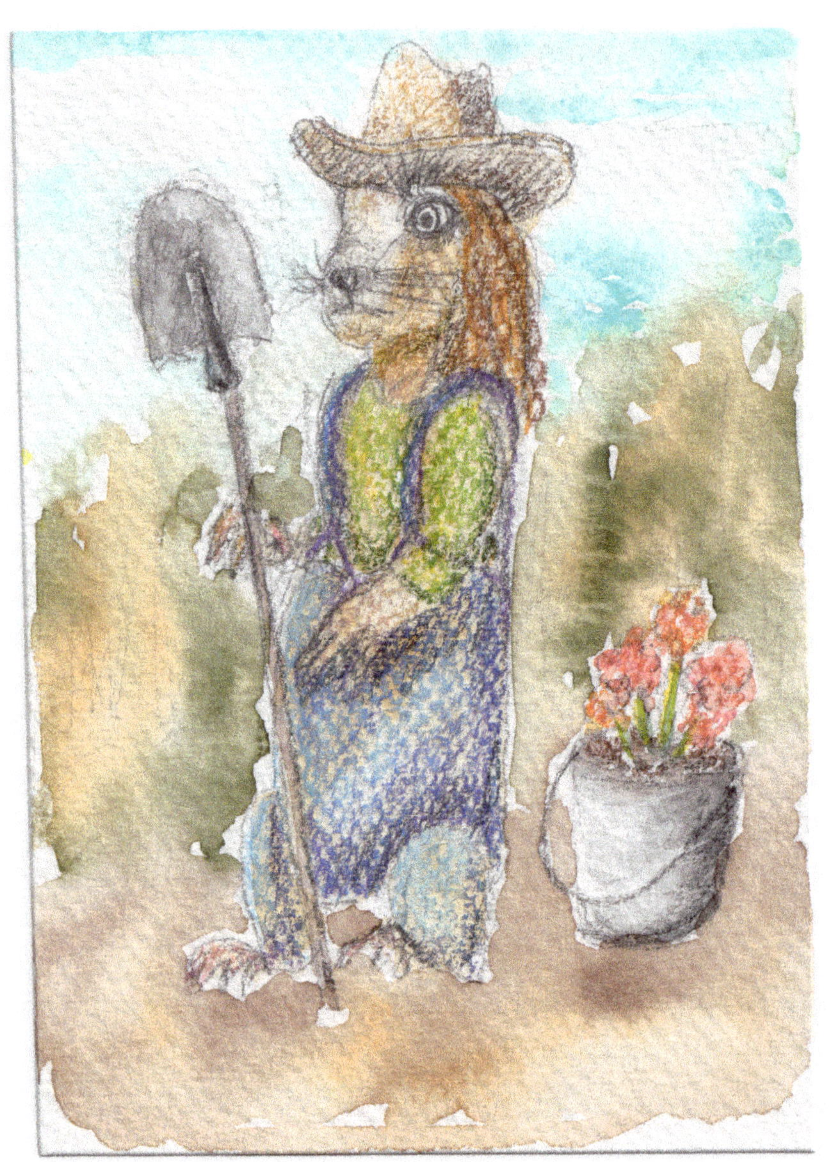

Weeding Our Garden

Our soul is our garden. A mysterious and magical place that provides a lifetime of wonders and miracles ready to bloom at any given point and time. Prairie dogs, like gardeners, aerate and fertilize the soil to help plants thrive. Similarly, we need to weed our soul garden if we want flowers to grow.

Of course, we could use a quick-fix chemical to kill off the weeds, like the abundantly available pharmaceuticals that we impulsively reach for to offer us relief. Chemicals damage or kill many non-weeds and potential buds waiting to blossom beneath the surface. By getting down to the source and closely examining the ground of our soul, we can begin to decipher that which we want to remove and that which we want to keep.

Through the use of gardening tools designed to remove the weeds at their roots, we can critically scrutinize each plant. This is dirty and hard work. But if we take a shortcut and only pull out what's visible on the surface, the weed removal will be temporary and most likely grow back doubled in strength.

Gardening enables us to make visible the beautiful flowers of our souls that would otherwise be strangled by weeds, the negative thoughts, feelings, and experiences we harbor. By removing their deep tangled grasps, we make visible the blossoming and evolving garden of our soul. If we choose not to put forth the effort of a consistent weeding practice, we will one day realize, unfortunately often when it's too late, that the beauty of our garden, who we are, has been inundated by weeds, and our soul has been strangled.

So, gather your shovel, bucket, tools, and hat. Discover what's underneath the weeds waiting and wanting to bloom in your soul!

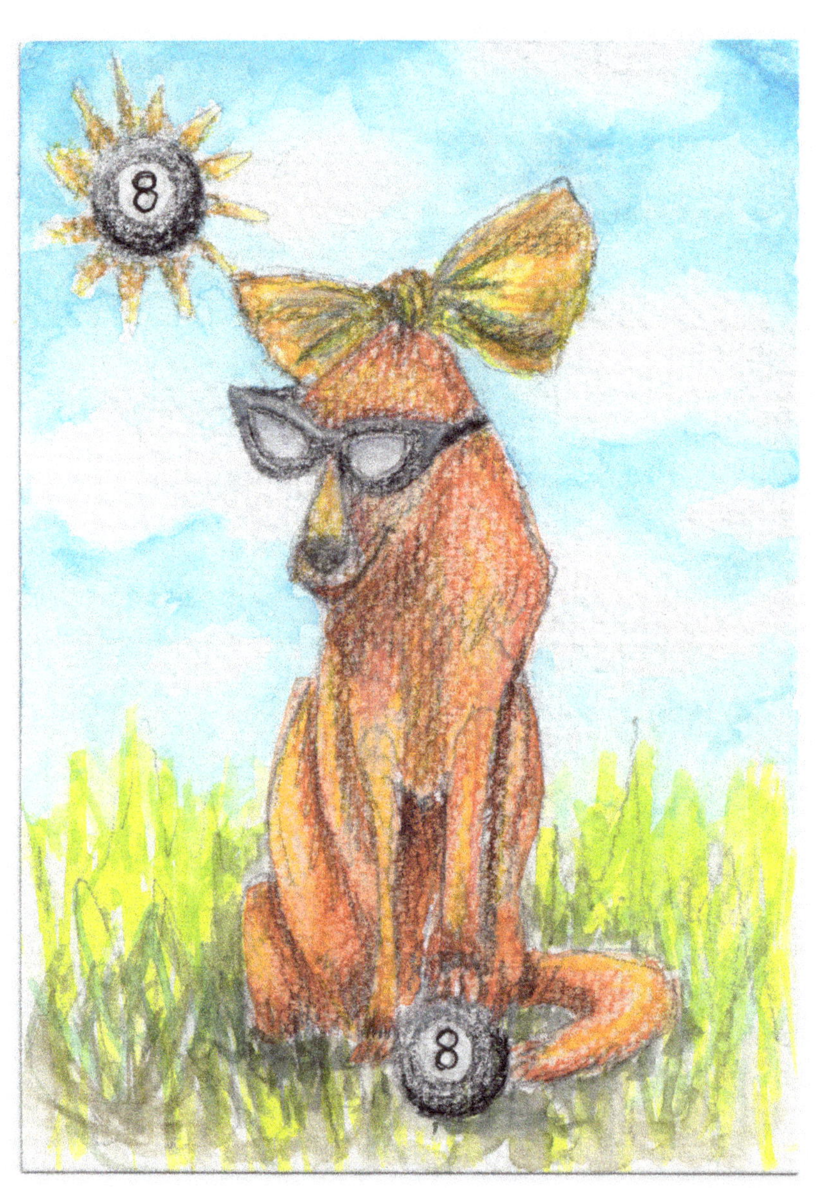

Signs and Symbols

The fox, a spiritual symbol of intuition, can be a sign that something is amiss when seen during the day. The 8-ball, a symbol of luck, can mean good and bad luck. How we interpret the things we experience is largely influenced by our own perception. How we see things at any given moment is determined by the glasses we wear and the lens through which we look. Like sunglasses that reflect what's in front of them, experiences placed before us reflect who we are, what we think and feel, and our energy. The law of attraction teaches us like attracts like.

When a fox crosses our path in the daytime, do we see this experience as a validation and encouragement to trust our intuition, or do we become filled with fear because we risk being attacked by a wild animal? Our reaction has less to do with the actual neutral stimuli of seeing a fox but rather what we bring to the experience as reflected by our personal beliefs and stories.

The reflective quality of sunglasses empowers us to engage in a world filled with meaningful depth and serendipity rather than a world ridden with superficial notions of chance. When we leave our life to chance by looking to a magic 8-ball fortune teller for answers, we forsake the power of personal choice. By consciously recognizing that the experiences and people reflected in our sunglasses are symbols and signposts that offer guidance, we empower ourselves to be the creators of our good fortune.

So go ahead, take a risk, and remove your sunglasses. Allow yourself to be lightened and enlightened. The universe is waiting to shine good fortune and new perspectives upon you!

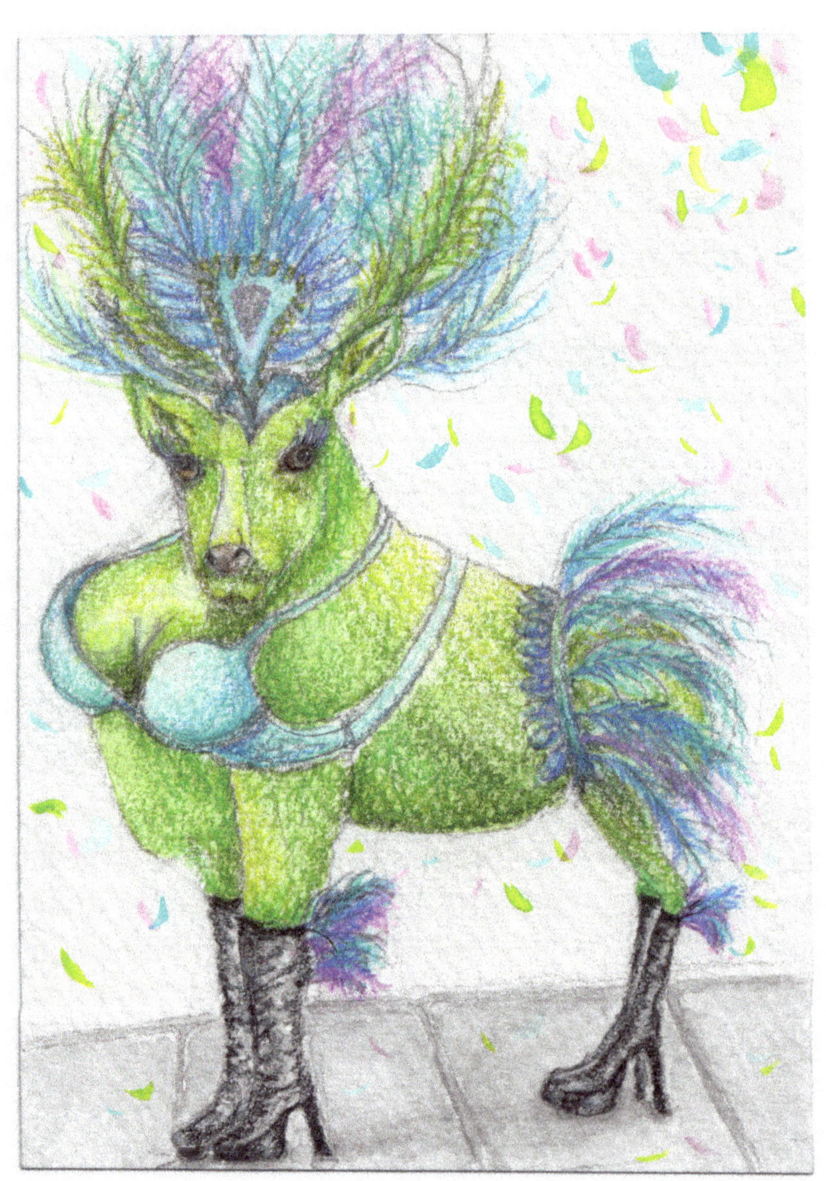

Carnival Queen

Some days feel like a carnival, festive and full of joy, while others are quite the opposite. What all days have in common, festive or not, is that they are an opportunity to live our life! It's the one chance we have at being who we were destined to be! Elks, symbolic of inner strength and passion, remind us to stay our course, be strong and steady, and live our best life.

Too often, unfortunately, we find ourselves listening to limiting messages, both from others and ourselves. They tell us, oh no, you shouldn't do this; someday…; oh I can't; or when…then… We tend to heed these messages rather than embracing opportunities in the here and now with a big, exuberant YES! Having only one shot at being us, why not live each day as an experience waiting to unfold and evolve? A chance to discover and share who we are and why we are here in this form and in this life.

We all have a purpose, a reason, for being here. Be curious, like a spectator at a carnival parade. Find the people, the outfits, and the colors that appeal to you and catch your intuitive eye. Be like the carnival queen and expose, parade, and celebrate yourself. Invite those around you to join the party. Let go of inhibitions, restrictions, and limiting beliefs. Allow yourself to be swept away in the flow of the life parade. Deck yourself out in the finest, most extravagant garments and connect with your amazingness. As you dance on the path of your journey, inspire and invite others to come along because YOU are the chosen carnival queen!

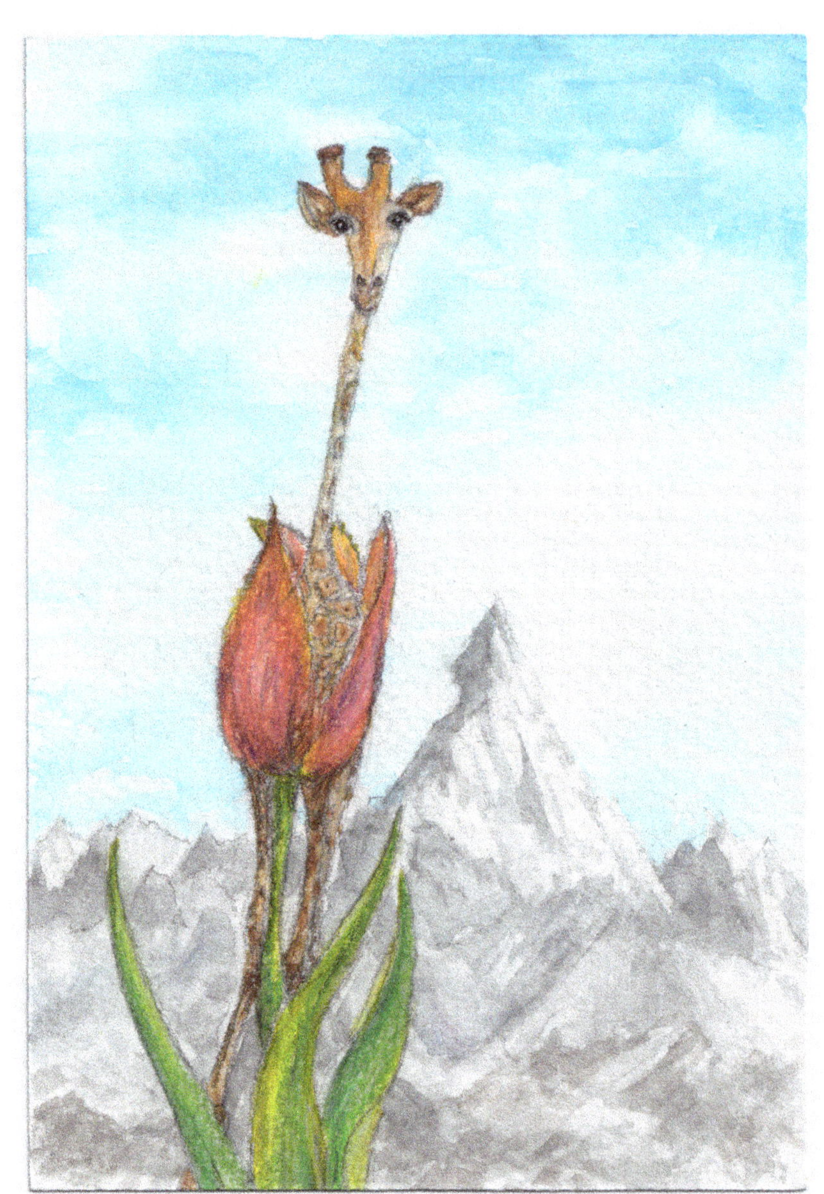

Standing Tall in Tadasana

Tadasana, translated as Mountain Pose, is a yoga āsana, or "pose." Standing upright with feet and hands facing forward appears deceitfully easy. However, when properly executed, it is far more challenging than one would expect. This pose, offering health benefits such as improved posture, is also the starting point for several additional standing yoga postures. A foundational root pose from which all else grows.

Tadasana offers us the opportunity to connect with ourselves through a steady and easy breath. Furthermore, it helps us to remember that by deeply rooting down, we can extend upwards and grow, becoming who we were put on this earth to be. Like a giraffe, we are here on this earth to stand tall unapologetically. Resembling a perennial tulip in springtime, radiating color vibrancy, we're here to grow, blossom, and shine our magnificence year, after year, after year.

Whether in line at the grocery store, giving the speech of a lifetime, or holding a loved one in your arms, stand upright with your feet facing forward and parallel to each other. Stack your hips, knees, and ankles over one another and put your pelvis in a neutral position. Pull your sternum towards the ceiling and keep your shoulders open, down, and away from your ears. Relax your arms and allow them to extend gently alongside your body. Balance the crown of your head directly over your pelvis. Soften your eyes and take a deep breath in and release a deep breath out.

With every inhalation and exhalation, you activate prana and connect with your life force energy. And as you breathe, you remember and return to who you truly are. You find peace knowing that the only place you need to be right in this moment is here and now. Standing tall and beautiful, unapologetically on this earth, with the strength and presence of the highest mountain, thriving with vigor and freshness of a springtime bloom. You are strong, perfect, whole, and beautiful, JUST AS YOU ARE!

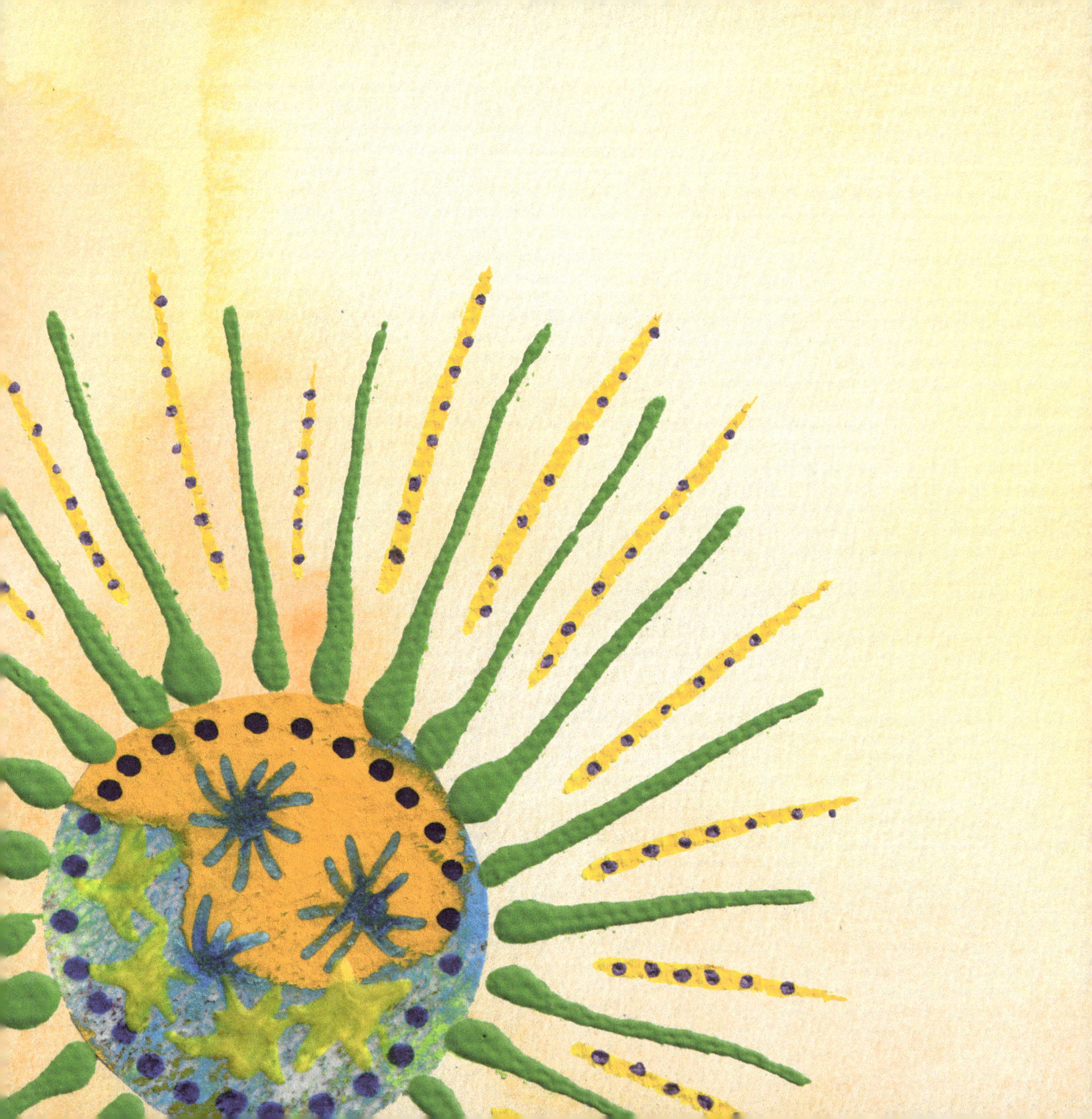

The following story is in honor of my father.

It is the 51st story of *Soul Bubbles*, which like his death,
unexpectedly became a part of my book and my life.

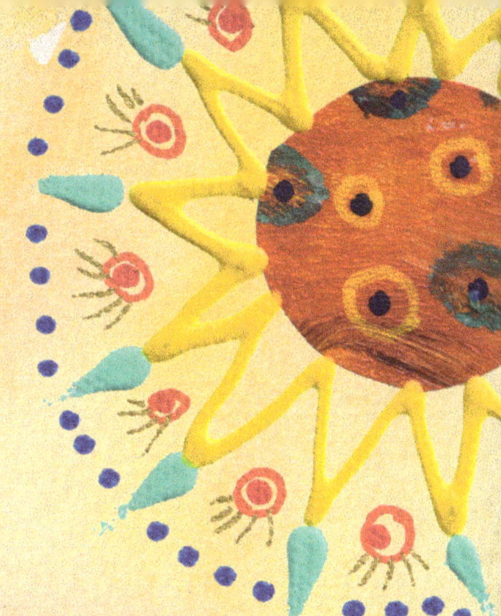

In Loving Memory of

Wolfgang Fürst

November 23, 1938 - October 29, 2022

The Power of Forgiveness

Trigger Warning: This story contains content about suicide.

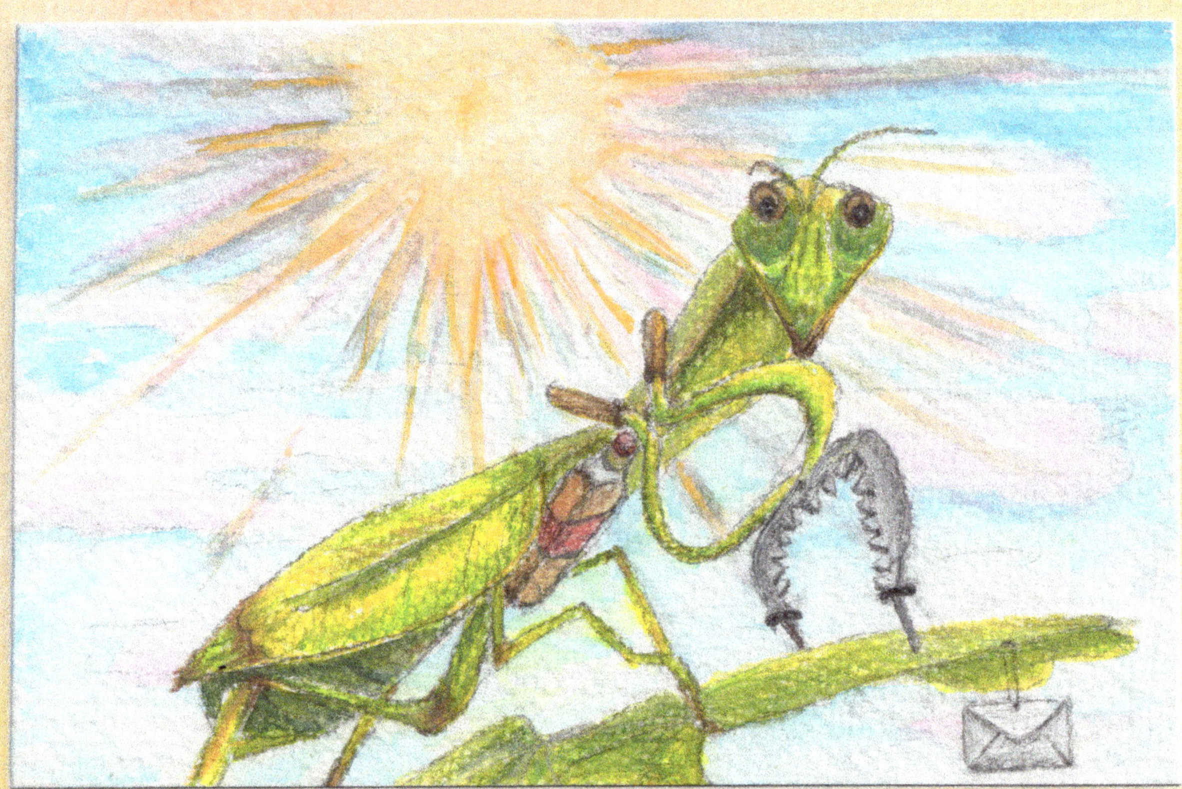

    According to spirit animal wisdom, the praying mantis comes to us when we are desperately in need of peace, quiet, and calm in our life. My father found peace, quiet, and calm when he took his own life, leaving behind a wake of chaos and turmoil for all those who love him. The death of my father happened in the midst of writing this book - right between the second and third drafts to be exact. Needless to say, my life and my book came to an abrupt halt as grief flooded my heart, filled my head, and dominated my waking hours.

It was during this intense time filled with loss and grief that the praying mantis came as a messenger from deep within my aching soul. Navigating amidst the circling and spinning thoughts and feelings of my head and heart, he ascended, finding his way to the surface, filled with strength, light, and wisdom. Accompanying me on the dark and confusing journey of grieving, the praying mantis became my healing companion, illuminating and giving clarity along the way.

And so it came to be that life gave rise to the praying mantis messenger, the unexpected 51st story of *Soul Bubbles* and my life. Although the original 50 animals continue to accompany me on my life journey, none of them spoke to the issue of death. Why would they? I had never experienced the death of a father, one of the most important people in my world. But just when I needed it most, the praying mantis emerged carrying the following message: *Healing is all about forgiveness, and forgiveness is found through the healing power of letting go*. By letting go and forgiving the deceased and ourselves, we create space in which the seed for healing can be planted. Nurturing the seed and trusting the process, our broken heart intuitively knows that one day this seemingly tiny little seed will blossom into something far more magnificent and stronger than we can possibly imagine in this time of grieving. The heart knows that this feeling of wholeness it so desperately yearns for will once again be ours.

Fear, power, and our need for control often cause us to maintain a fierce grip, like fire tongs, on that which means the most to us - those we love and the life we share. Silently battling the isolation of his inner and outer worlds, ideals and reality, the walking canes that once assisted and eased mobility were no longer enough. Safely tucking a bottle tightly under his wing, the whisky served as a necessary elixir of courage to do what he felt he needed to do - to take that last step, that final independent step, to ultimate and limitless freedom. Teetering on the brink for probably longer than he ever communicated or any of us realized, the river's edge on that sunny fall day served as his portal. And as he let go, his final words, written on an envelope, asked for forgiveness. It was then that the correlation between letting go and forgiving became clear.

And as the praying mantis leapt from the leaf, the rays of the sun illuminated his way. Becoming one with the glistening sparkles of sunlight on the water's gentle waves, the praying mantis submerged into eternal peace, calm, and quiet.

"Where there is sun, you will find me. When you turn your face to the sun, I will kiss your forehead. Through the warmth of the rays, you will feel and know in your heart that you are not alone. I am always here with you, for I am okay, happy, and finally free."

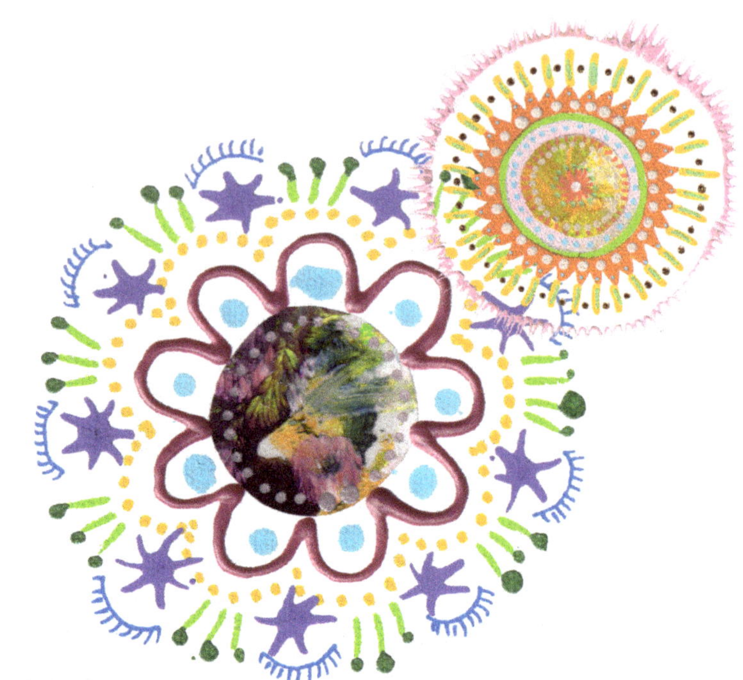
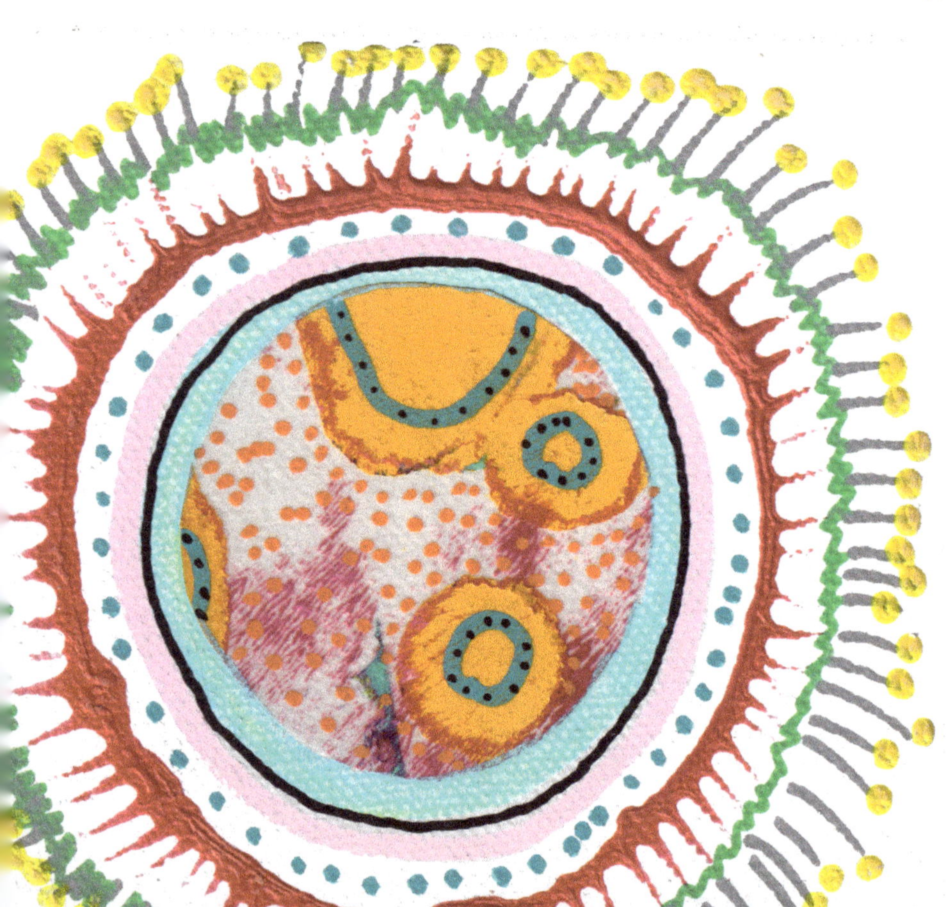

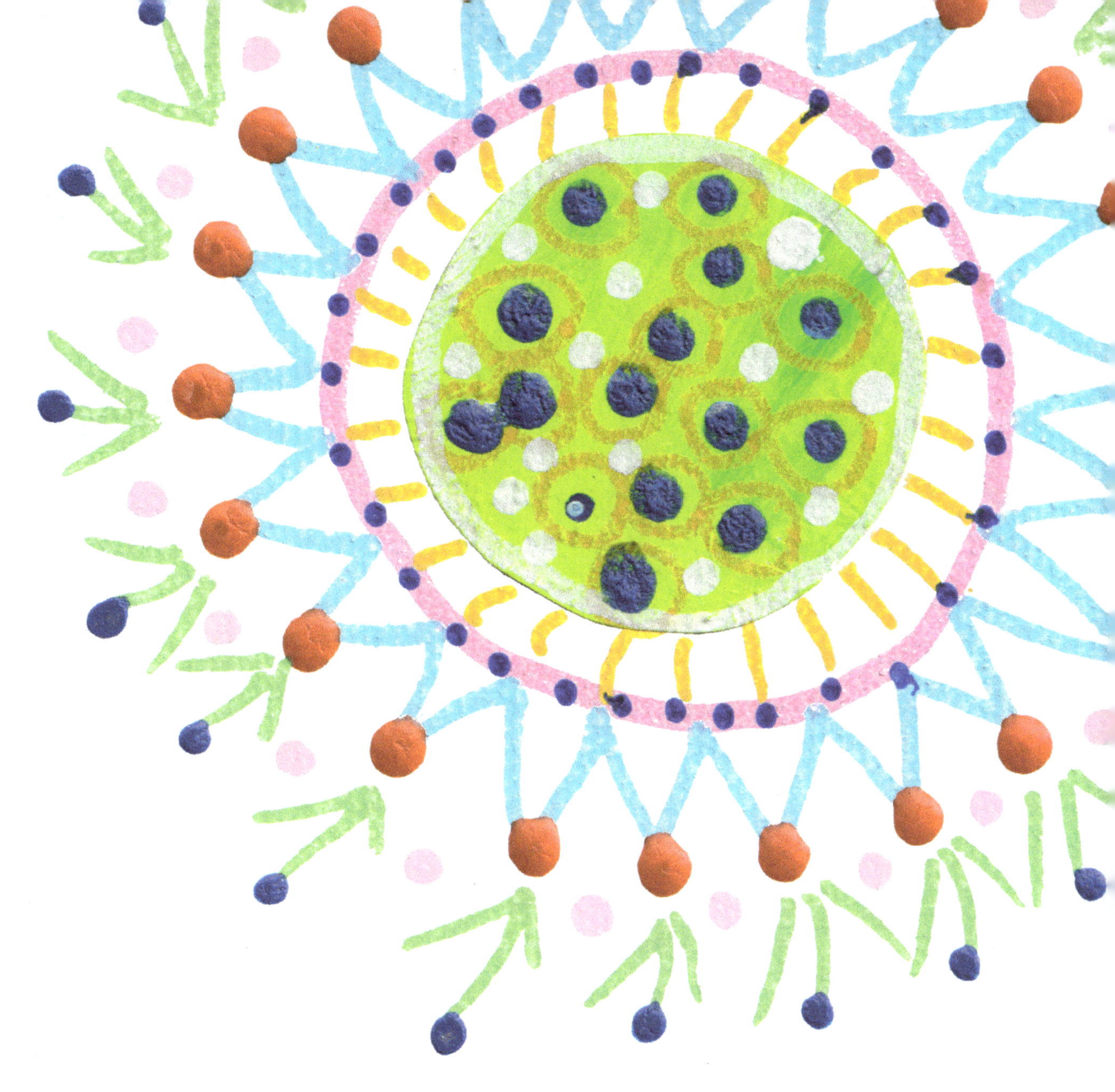

Animal Tribute

It is with heartfelt gratitude that I would like to honor the animals who appeared to me in both my inner and outer worlds. Always with the most serendipitous timing, carrying the message I needed to receive in a particular moment, they are the inspiration for *Soul Bubbles*. Thank you for being and accompanying me on my life journey.

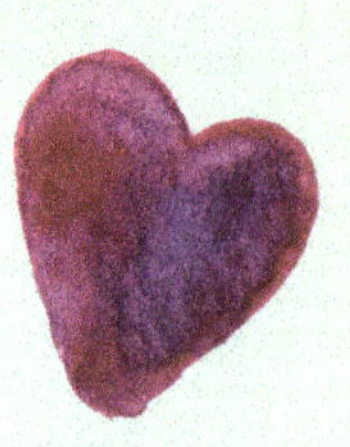

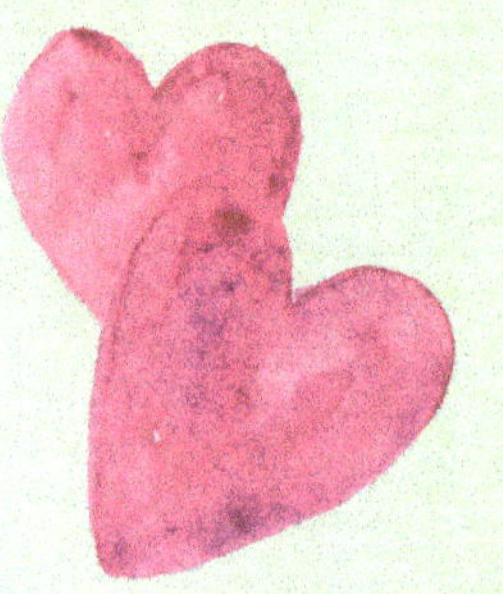

TURTLE teacher basking in the sun down at the neighborhood pond.
The **RABBIT** I encountered on an afternoon run in the woods.
The **ZEBRAS** of Robert M. Sapolsky's research and book *Why Zebras Don't Get Ulcers*.
Our backyard **BIRDS** whose melodious morning songs serve as a daily wake-up and tune-in call.
The smiling **CRABS** on the moonlit beach of the Outer Banks in North Carolina, USA.
The **DOLPHINS** in the Adriatic for sharing their playful spirits with us on sailing trips.
The **WOODPECKER** in our backyard, resiliently seeking nourishment in all seasons of life.
The **SWANS** of my childhood fairytales.
The **OWL** surfacing to celebrate the graduations of my nephews Andrew and Matthew.
All the circus **ELEPHANTS** who benevolently bring joy to others.
The inspiring **BEAVERS** in Thaya National Park, Austria, for their dam-building perseverance.
The **FISH** within me who surfaces when I feel out of place.
My inner yoga **MOUSE**, giving me peace and connection.
The broken-wing **BUTTERFLY** I held in my hand while on a trek to Machu Picchu in Peru.
My personal overeating inner **SLOTH** tendencies.
The solitary and balanced **FLAMINGO** inside me.
The **DOG** on my childhood "I Hate Mondays" poster.
The Mixed-Up **CHAMELEON**, one of my all-time favorite books by Eric Carle.
My childhood stuffed animal **MONKEY** Affie, still with me today, wearing his overall suit.
The tiny glass **PORCUPINE** sculpture on my father's nightstand, a gift from my mother during their time of courting.
Randy the **HERON** who majestically graces me during post-run stretches at the pond.
Summertime **LADYBUGS** bestowing the feeling of good fortune upon me.
The innumerable **TURKEYS** sacrificing their lives for Thanksgiving celebrations.

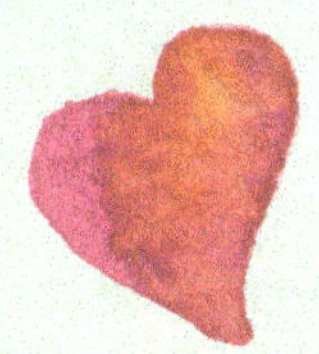
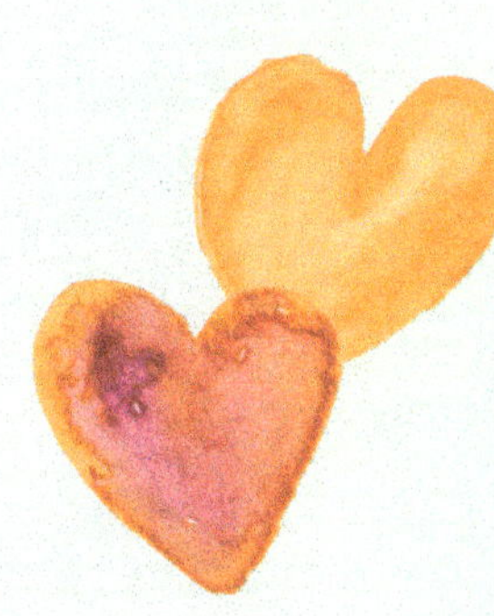

The **MAYFLY** fluttering from my soul when I take myself and life too seriously.

The **CHICKEN** that inspired me to ask the supermarket clerk, "did they have a good life?"

The emotionally expansive **PUFFERFISH** inside of me.

My inner stubborn and doubting **BULL**.

Sweet labrador **DOG** Layla, who came into the world and our life on March 17, 2022.

The **FROG** within me, whose eyes could not believe that 27 years had passed when my friend Mary's daughter announced her wedding.

Milk **COWS** and my friend Meg for the permission to have cereal for dinner.

The strong and persevering **SALMON** we saw while hiking along the levadas on Madeira Island, Portugal.

The **SQUIRRELS** in our backyard whose behavior lets me know when seasons are changing.

The colony of **ANTS** in my childhood glass ant farm.

The **PIG** whose gaze from the slaughter truck window opened my eyes to a vegetarian lifestyle.

The **BEAR** strolling around my cabin in the woods of Colorado, USA.

The **PEACOCK** who crossed the road as we departed from a family gathering, that unbeknownst to us at the time, would be our last visit with Dad before he died.

The partying **MOLE** in my aunt Steffi's garden.

The relentless effort and hard work of a **BEE** colony we cohabitated with one summer.

The **LIONESS** within me, a manifestation of my Leo star sign.

The **SHEEP** figurines in my husband Peter's memorabilia collection.

The bald **EAGLE**, a national symbol of my home away from home, America.

Franz Marc's blue **HORSE** paintings I often visited at the MoMA in NYC.

My niece Alex and her **DOG** Lucy for making "mama jeans" memories with me.

The **HIPPOPOTAMUS** residing in the sometimes exhausted hippocampus of my brain.

My inner feminine **KANGAROO** celebrating the maternal instincts of childbearing and non-childbearing women alike.

The **BOARS** I sometimes encounter on late evening runs in the Vienna woods.

The **PRAIRIE DOGS** living in the grasslands of my former home state, Colorado, USA.

The **FOX** I serendipitously met on a rare daytime run.

The **ELK** and their bugling parties I experienced in Colorado, USA.

My inner **GIRAFFE**, personifying the phrase "standing unapologetically" spoken by my yoga teacher and friend Jess.

The **PRAYING MANTIS** who joined me on the journey of healing shortly after the death of my father.

The bathing **OTTER** who serendipitously swam onto the cover of *Soul Bubbles* during the book design process.

Love and Gratitude

Illustrating and writing a book was not one of the items on my life "To-Do" list. Rather, it was a process that evolved and unfolded gently and naturally over time. Looking back with hindsight, it was more like a beautiful string of events, a pearl necklace, that although seemingly unconnected at the time, were all necessary parts of the journey that brought me to this very moment - writing the acknowledgments for my first to be published book.

While some pearls on the necklace know who they are and are aware of their role, others will learn through this book the influence they had. And there are some pearls cited here whose influence is unbeknownst to them. But isn't that also true in life - often, we never know the effect(s) we have on others, the imprint we leave on their hearts, the blueprints of life. Whether intentional or unintentional, it is with the utmost gratitude that I cite my dearest pearls below. We are all connected, and may gratitude unite us in this celebration of *Soul Bubbles*.

First and foremost, I would like to thank my biggest fan, confidant, sounding board, beta reader, best friend, partner, husband, and love of my life, Peter, for inspiring, supporting, and always believing in me. Your authentic and honest expression of delight as I shared each piece with you heartened me to continue and complete this project. Thank you for being my anchor, my harbor, and the best darn skipper to navigate this book journey and life with! I LOVE YOU!

Thank you to my parents, Wolfgang and Hannelore, because without them, I would not be here. And although I have spent much of my life trying to figure out which one I am most like, I am learning more and more every day that I am the best of both. I am who and how I am because of you, and for that, I am truly and deeply grateful!

To my engineering-minded brother Klaus, who coined the phrase *Soul Bubbles* that then became the title and heart of this book. Thank you for always creating and holding a safe space of unconditional love in which I could be my authentic self and let my deep thoughts bubble to the surface.

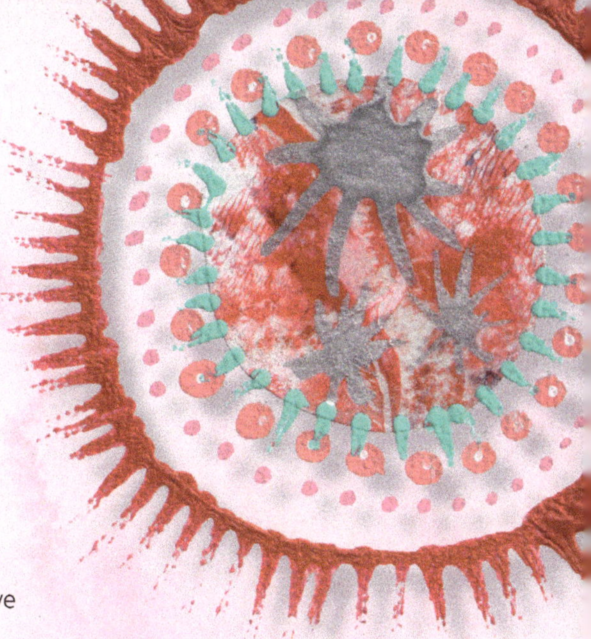

My beta readers, Colette, Mary, and Sherri, for taking the time out of their busy lives to meet, sit, engage, reflect, and respond to the 50 animals from a place of authenticity. Your trusted, genuine, and constructive feedback encouraged and moved this book from good to great.

Sage Adderley, my writing coach and support for all things book and non-book related on my writing journey.

Monica LoCascio, my book fairy extraordinaire, for sprinkling her magical dust of creativity and wisdom on this book and bringing it to life.

Lex Thompson, who captured the beautiful moments of being my creative, joyful, playful Self on camera.

Alex, Meg, Mary Beth and everyone else (including you, dear reader) whose enthusiasm and support have accompanied and inspired me on this book journey and in life.

Jessica Patterson, teacher and friend, whose yogic wisdom is woven into the fabric of my being and reflected in the bubbles of my soul.

Karen Abend, whose 30-day creativity challenge was the initial inspiration for the animal drawings.

Carla Sonheim and her playful continuous blind contour lessons that moved my inner critic aside, freeing me up to hear the voices of the animals and visualize the stories they have to share.

Liz Tran, whose artwork and art class taught me the technique of creating bedazzled circles.

Berthild Zeirl, my Austrian art teacher, whose 6+ years of continuous watercolor and drawing instruction gave me the skills and confidence to make and share my art. Her words of "Trau dich nur" (Trust yourself) will forever be imprinted in my heart.

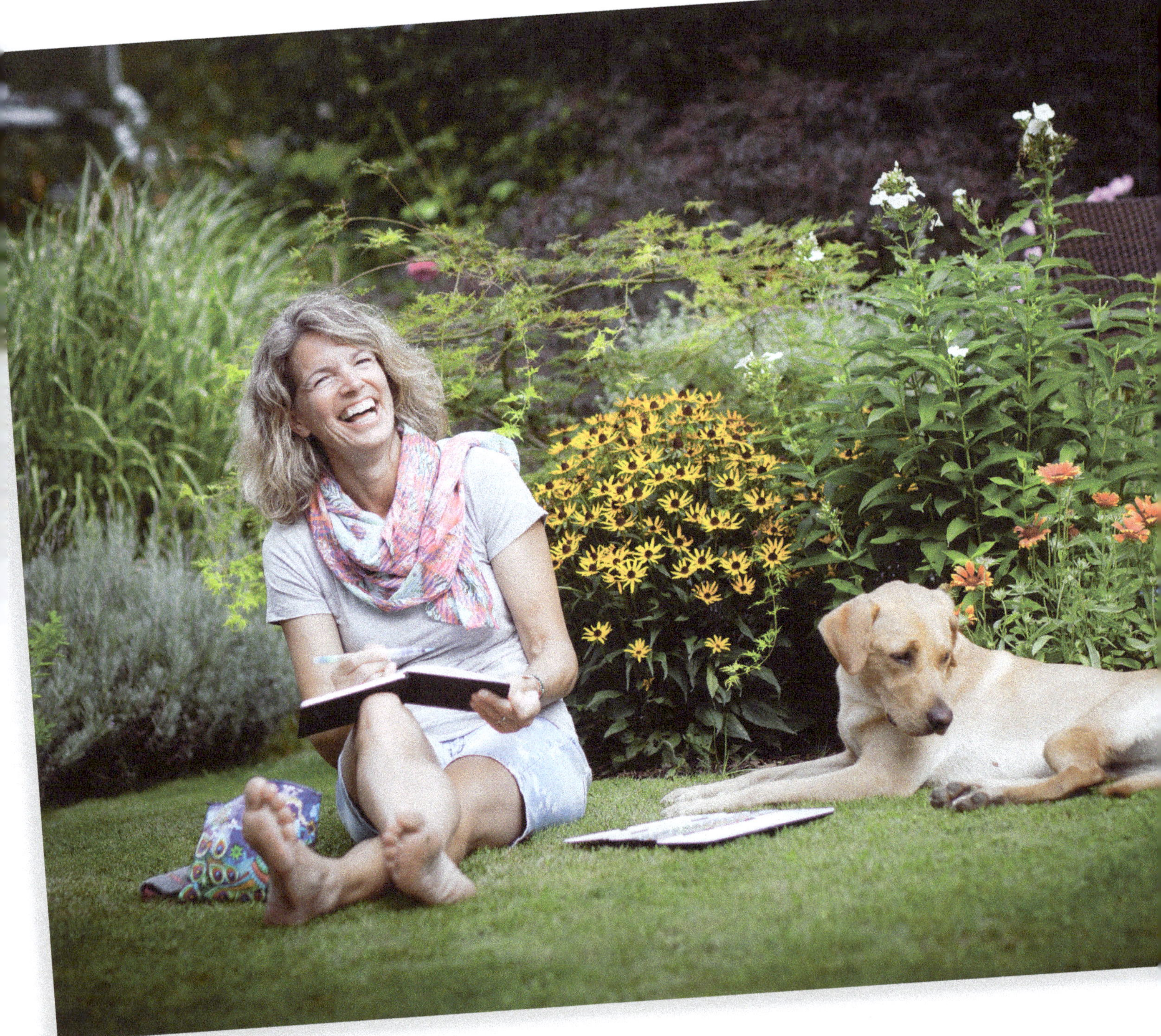

A Bubble About Sabina

Sabina Mesaric is a licensed art educator and registered art therapist currently living and teaching elementary art in Vienna, Austria. Born in Munich, Germany, and spending the majority of her life in the United States, she considers herself a Bavarian-American. In addition to sharing her love of art with others, she enjoys spending time in nature - running, hiking, camping, and sailing with her husband, Peter, and labrador, Layla. Sabina can also be found playing in her art studio; on her yoga mat; digging in her garden; sipping coffee and pondering all things life, or simply being.

For as long as she can remember, Sabina has always felt and sought the deeper meaning of things. Now, at 52, she is honoring and celebrating her way of being, giving rise to and making tangible the intangible thoughts and feelings residing deep within. *Soul Bubbles* is the expression of her rich inner life, an innate gift she attributes to being a highly sensitive person (HSP).

Through her playful approach to real-life topics, she takes the reader on a beautiful and thought-provoking visual and literary journey while presenting the inherent wisdom of each message in a relatable and enjoyable way for readers.

You can find Sabina on her website at www.yogartsoul.com

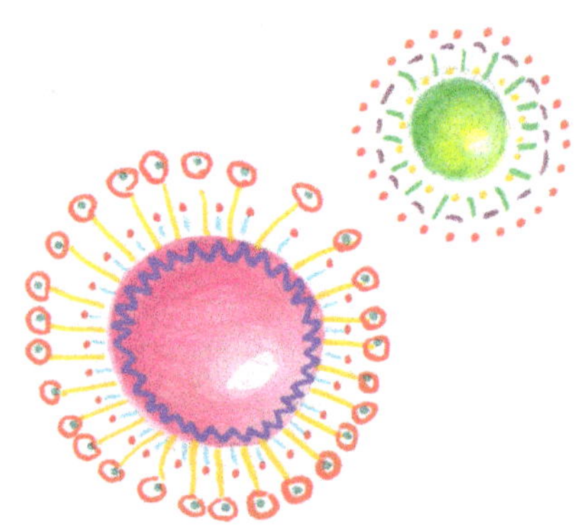